Quiltmaker's Guide to Fine Machine Appliqué

By Karla Menaugh & Cherie Ralston
Foreword and Patterns by Barbara Brackman

SUNFLOWER PATTERN CO-OPERATIVE

Author's note

Authors:
Karla Menaugh & Cherie Ralston
Foreword & Patterns:
Barbara Brackman
Photography:
Jon Blumb

Published by
Sunflower Pattern Co-operative
PMB#C-237, 3115 W. Sixth Street
Lawrence, KS 66049

First edition, first printing
ISBN: 0-9725457-0-0

Printed in the United States of America by Boelte-Hall Litho, Inc., Roeland Park, Kansas

For many years, I was one of those quiltmakers who thought I would never be able to make an appliquéd quilt. A fused joint in my right thumb denied me the dexterity to produce nice needle-turn appliqué. Raw-edge appliqué and satin-stitched edges were not acceptable alternatives to me; I wanted to make heirloom-quality appliqué quilts with turned-edge appliqué and plenty of tiny, nearly invisible stitches. That's when Cherie Ralston changed my quilting life.

Cherie is one of those people who is always looking for a better way to do things. In the early 1990s, she tried all the popular machine appliqué techniques, many based on the blind hem stitch. She then searched the stitch selections on her Bernina sewing machine for a stitch that would be less visible, yet sturdy. She settled on the Variable Overlock stitch, overriding the stitch length and width settings until the stitch was very narrow and short. Then she tried various threads, finally choosing a two-ply, 50-weight cotton thread that blends into the yarns of the appliqué fabric.

Cherie's techniques included preparing the appliqué shapes on freezer paper with edges turned under and glued. When I tried my first quilt, I found that I was finally able to produce the kind of appliqué that I had dreamed about. When I showed my quilts to others, they often were surprised to learn that they had been stitched on the machine. I think the most telling story is from Anne Thomas, who hand-quilted *War & Pieces,* one of our early Sunflower Pattern Co-operative designs. She had been quilting for about a month when I happened to mention the machine appliqué to her. She was shocked! Even though she had been looking at the quilt close-up for many hours each day, she still had not noticed the machine stitching.

For me, this technique isn't just about saving time, although most people will find they can machine appliqué faster than they can hand appliqué. It's about gaining enough control over the appliqué shapes and the stitching to produce a beautiful, sturdy quilt.

by Karla Menaugh

Lesson 8
— Combined Techniques

Contents

Lesson 1
— Outer Curves, Layering

Lesson 9
— Strip-Pieced Leaves

The Machine and The Quilt

From the Eighteenth Century to the Twenty-first

By Barbara Brackman, author of *The Encyclopedia of Pieced Quilt Blocks, Encyclopedia of Appliqué, Clues in the Calico,* and *Patterns of Progress: Quilts in the Machine Age*

From the earliest sewing machine—-the model made for Thomas Saint's original British patent in 1790 — machines were designed to make quilts. Early machines came with quilting attachments, and as soon as machines made their way into American homes, women began using their Singers, their New Homes and their Wheeler and Wilson machines to quilt the layers together. They also used the machine stitch to piece designs and to anchor appliqué patches as well as to assemble the quilt and bind it.

America's first practical sewing machine was patented by Walter Hunt. His 1834 model featured a needle with an eye at the point. Another innovation was the interlocked stitch, locking two threads into a continuous seam. The story is told that Hunt's daughter, who realized the machine's potential, worried that it would deprive female seamstresses of their only livelihood. The altruistic Hunt abandoned his invention. Ten years later, Elias Howe Jr. re-invented Hunt's double-threaded machine with the eye at the needle's point. Howe received royalties of $25 for every American machine sold for the first few decades, one reason the prices were as high as $125.

Sewing machines made dramatic alterations in women's lives. No longer a human "sewing machine," a woman's daily work changed as did her education. Girls born before 1860 spent their childhood and adolescence learning to sew a fine hand. The evidence of their education is in their quilts, especially in the appliquéd extravaganzas made before the Civil War. Once the machine was widely available, hand skills steadily declined. Initially, quilters were proud to show off their machine work. They mixed machine and hand quilting in the same quilt. Their hand-pieced basket quilts often featured machine-appliquéd handles. Today's traditionalists are confused when they see these obvious machine stitches, but in the days when the machine was new and a luxury, the machine stitch was considered quite attractive.

The price of machines dropped as the competition increased. By 1880, 124 American manufacturers made machines, many of them long-forgotten lines named Little Wonder and Little Worker, New Boston and New Buckeye, the Fairy, The Gem and the Ten Dollar Novelty. We've recalled some of the fanciful machine names in the patterns for our *New Century Garden* and *New Century Sampler.*

As machines became more commonplace during the early 20th century, quiltmakers began to feel they must hide their machine stitches in the construction. Hand work became the standard for visible appliqué and quilting. Machine-appliquéd or machine-quilted pieces were considered less attractive, less valuable and finally less authentic. Exhibits at fairs and contests developed categories specifically for machine-quilted or machine-appliquéd pieces. That division continues today, dividing hand work and machine work into two categories, separate but still not equal.

In 1989 Caryl Bryer Fallert's quilt *Corona II: The Solar Eclipse* won the top prize at the American Quilters' Society's prestigious show in Paducah, Kentucky. Competing against hand-quilted work in a show known for its conservative attitude, Fallert's machine-quilted piece won a $10,000 purchase prize. Suddenly quilters began looking at their machines from a new perspective. Some artists flaunt the machine stitch, reveling in the look, while other contemporary innovators use the machine to imitate the look of hand sewing.

In the 1980s, Jeri Hoffmeyer and Marie Shirer described in a *Quilters Newsletter Magazine* article the basics of an imitation hand-appliqué technique with a blind hemstitch and fusible interfacing. Over the years, teachers and writers have modified the technique, developing new tricks using different stitches, different threads and different stiffening materials from spray starch to freezer paper. The technique we describe is one we've adapted and revised until we feel it's perfect. It's quick, accurate, and almost invisible, methods that will change the way you think about quiltmaking in the New Century.

Sewing Machine Requirements

We both use Berninas, Cherie a 930 and Karla an 1130. Each has a great stitch called the Vari-Overlock that can be made very narrow and very short. We'll talk more about that on page 8.

Most Berninas have the Vari-Overlock and allow the user to override the stitch settings infinitely, a "must" for setting up a very narrow stitch. But you can use this technique on any machine that has a zig-zag stitch, as long as the machine will allow you to adjust the stitch length and width to make the zig-zag very narrow and short.

You're going to be depending on your machine to do a good job for you, so you must keep it in good working order. Clean and oil it regularly as you are sewing, and take it to the dealer for regular service checks.

Check the tension to be sure it is even. The fine, narrow stitching sometimes pulls the bobbin thread up to the top. When you do the tests we describe on page 8, check to see if little dots of bobbin thread are showing through on the top of your appliqué. If they are, you'll need to tighten your bobbin tension or slightly loosen the top tension. Check your owner's manual.

Other machine requirements

- **Needles:** Size 70 sharp needles. Put in a new needle at the start of each new project. Change needles if you notice snagging or other problems. Sometimes even new needles can have imperfections that can interfere with good stitching. Don't hesitate to replace a needle that is causing problems.
- **Presser foot:** You will need an open-toe or clear plastic appliqué foot so that you can watch your stitching. We use Bernina's #37 patchwork foot. It has a long narrow opening in front that allows us to see our stitching clearly, and its long toes hold down the edges of our appliqué pieces.
- **Good light in front of the needle.** It's important to make the narrowest stitch possible. We augment our machine lighting by placing a desk-size Ott-Lite right in front of the machine to light the area in front of the needle. The better you can see your stitching, the narrower you can make your machine stitch.
- **Needle Up/Needle Down lever (optional):** Some machines can be programmed to stop with the needle in the "up" or in the "down" position. If yours has this option, choose "down." This will keep the needle positioned correctly in your fabric whenever you need to stop and lift the presser foot to change sewing directions.
- **Knee-lift for the presser foot: (optional):** If you can use a knee lever to lift the presser foot, you can keep your hands on your appliqué project while lifting the foot to turn corners or steer around curves.

- **Mirror-image (optional):** The Variable Overlock stitch sews on the left side of the appliqué, a bit like driving on the left side of the road. If your machine has the Variable Overlock stitch but you prefer to sew on the right-hand side of the fabric, the mirror-image option will come in handy. No matter which stitch you use, the mirror-image function can make your sewing easier. If you become "ambidextrous," able to sew on either the right or left edge of the appliqué, you can switch sides and keep the bulk of your project on the left side of the machine, out of the way of the machine housing.

- **Thread:** The right thread is essential to the quality of the machine appliqué. We use DMC 50 machine embroidery (Broder Machine) all-cotton thread. This is a two-ply lightweight thread. Its dull finish blends right into the reproduction and primitive fabrics we often use.

  If you prefer a different brand, look for two-ply thread that is 50 or 60 weight. The higher the number of the weight, the thinner the thread. Other possible threads are Mettler 60 two-ply cotton thread or YLI silk thread. The YLI is a little shiny for working with reproduction fabrics but its shiny finish would blend well with batiks or bright fabrics.

  Plan to use the same thread in both the top and the bobbin of your machine. Don't stress about having to buy every color of thread. We buy grey and taupe thread in light, medium and dark shades and find that they blend into a variety of fabrics. We rarely buy green, blue or pink thread. Grey thread usually blends into green and blue fabrics and taupe often blends into the pinks. Eventually you'll need black, a couple of good reds, dark and medium brown (works for purple and red, too), a few cream-colored threads and a range of golds and rusts. To check a thread color, pull out one thread and lay it across the appliqué fabric to see how it blends.

  Don't try to use regular weight, three-ply or heavier threads. They are too heavy for the tiny machine stitch and will make your stitching much more visible.

Choosing a Machine Stitch That Mimics Hand Appliqué

The goal is to use a machine stitch that acts just like hand appliqué — taking a tiny bite into the edge of the appliqué 7 or 8 times per inch.

The stitch that looks the most like hand appliqué is the Variable Overlock. On most machines, it takes three straight stitches forward, then one zig-zag stitch followed by three more straight stitches and another zig-zag, etc. It is similar to the Blind Hem stitch, but the Variable Overlock is narrower and takes fewer stitches between bites. Another distinguishing characteristic is that it always bites from the left to the right, the opposite of the Blind Hem stitch.

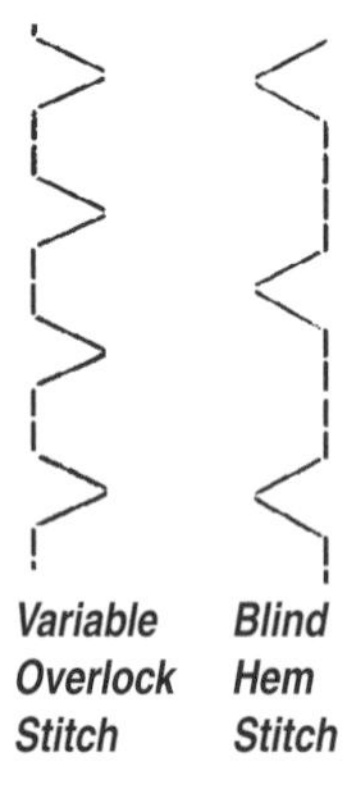

To make this stitch mimic hand appliqué, you will have to override the default settings to make it much narrower and shorter. All machine settings vary from model to model, even within the same brand. For the best setting on your machine, compare a stitched sample to the full-size samples shown.

- First, change the needle position to the "center."
- Change the stitch width to approximately 0.5 on a scale of 0 to 5.
- Change the stitch length to approximately 0.5, just a little longer than satin stitch.
- If your machine has a mirror-image feature, turn it on so you can stitch along the right side of the appliqué piece. Otherwise, you'll have to stitch on the left. Like driving in England, it can be done but takes a little getting used to!
- Other machine options: Set "Needle Up/Needle Down" to "Down." If you have a knee lever for lifting the presser foot, install it.

After you have made these changes, test the stitch width and length to find a setting that is exactly right for your machine.

- Fold a small scrap of fabric in half and place it on top of a scrap of contrasting fabric.
- Be sure your sewing area has good lighting. We usually put an Ott-Lite right in front of our machines so that we have extra light on the stitching area. If you wear glasses for reading or close work, wear them.
- Put DMC 50 or another fine, two-ply thread on the top and bobbin of your machine so you get a true idea of what your machine stitch will look like. Use different thread colors on the top and the bobbin so you can check the tension. Choose colors that contrast with your fabric so you can see the stitching. If your bobbin has an extra hole in its hook, thread it.

- Pretend the folded edge of the scrap fabric is the edge of the appliqué shape. Sew along the edge, with the straight stitches going "in the ditch" of the background fabric, right along the edge of the appliqué. The zig-zag stitch should bite into the appliqué fabric edge.
- Adjust your stitch width and length to match this sample for the least visible stitches:

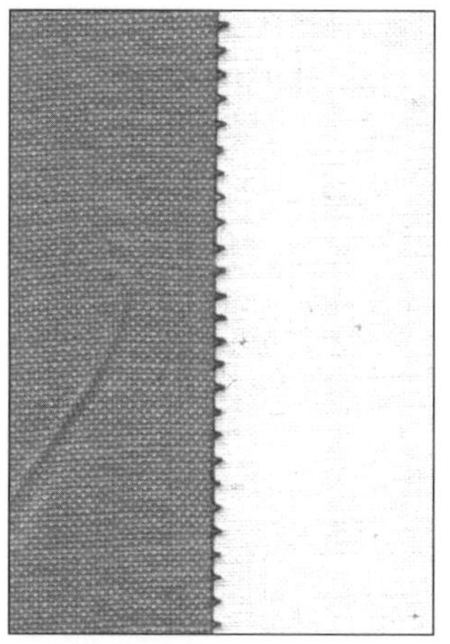

Front of narrow Vari-Overlock stitch. The white fabric has been appliquéd to the dark background.

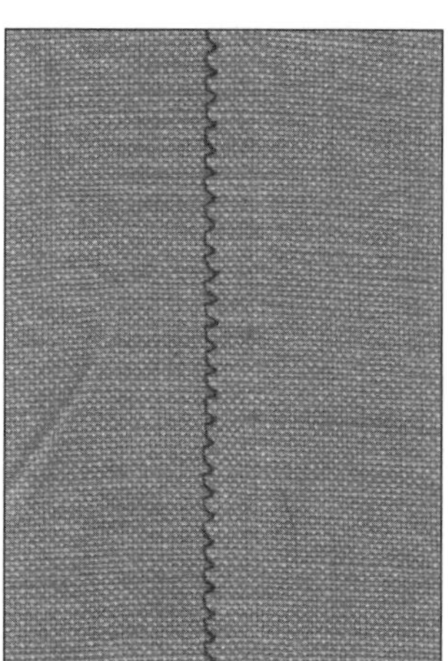

Back of narrow Vari-Overlock stitch.

- You may need to further adjust the stitch width to accommodate your eyesight and your machine settings. Karla's Bernina 1130 makes a perfect narrow stitch at 0.4 width, 0.5 length; Cherie's 930 makes a similar stitch at a width and length just under 1.

  Don't overlook the importance of accommodating your eyesight. It is critical to sew accurately. The straight stitches should go into the background fabric at the edge of the appliqué, and the zig-zag stitches should just nick the appliqué. If you find that the above stitch width is too difficult for you to follow as you're stitching, widen the stitch gradually until you find a setting that works. A slight difference will not be too noticeable on the finished quilt, but it may be much easier for you to control.

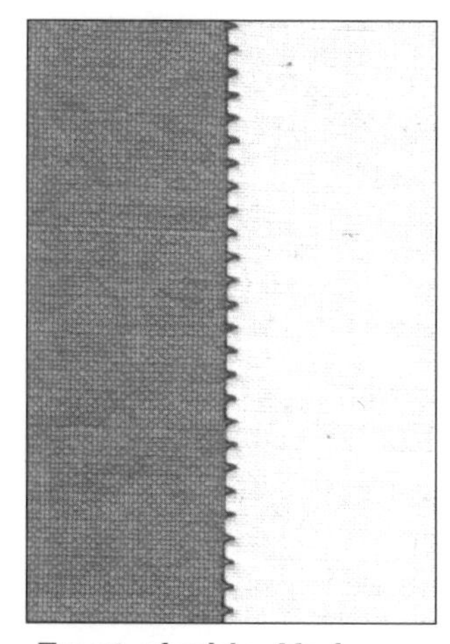

Front of wider Vari-Overlock stitch.

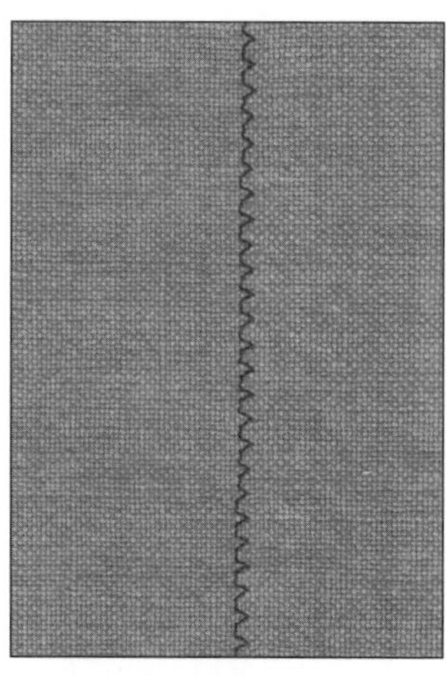

Back of wider Vari-Overlock stitch.

OPTIONS IF YOU CAN'T MAKE THIS STITCH WORK ON YOUR MACHINE

If you have a Bernina sewing machine, you will have no trouble. Most Berninas have the Variable Overlock stitch and will allow you to override the stitch width and length settings infinitely.

Some machines will not have the Variable Overlock stitch. Or, they may have a similar stitch but will limit how much the stitch settings can be overridden. Owners of those machines may end up with a stitch that is too wide or takes bites that are too far apart. In those cases, here are some options:

- If your machine has the Vari-Overlock stitch but you can't override the settings to make it narrow enough, try leaving a single needle in the machine but employing the double-needle option. In the double-needle setting, the stitch width is counted from the outside of the left needle to the outside of the right needle. If only one needle is installed, the stitch width is cut in half.
- Look for other stitches that will take only two or three straight stitches between bites. Maybe the blind-hem stitch will work on your machine. Or a feather stitch. It is better to choose stitches whose "bites" are in a "Vee" rather than a straight line. The straight-line bite doubles back on itself, and the resulting line of double-thread is more visible than the single thread in a "Vee" bite.
- Choose a narrow zig-zag stitch. Most machines have zig-zag, and most will allow the width and length to be adjusted infinitely. The width should be about 0.5 or whatever your eyesight will allow, and the length should be about 1.0 on a scale of 0-5. Compare your stitching to this actual-size sample.

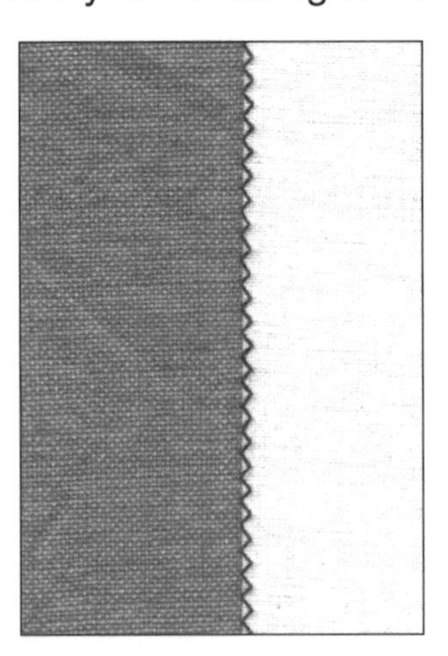

Zig-zag: Width: 1.0, length: 1.0 on a Bernina 930

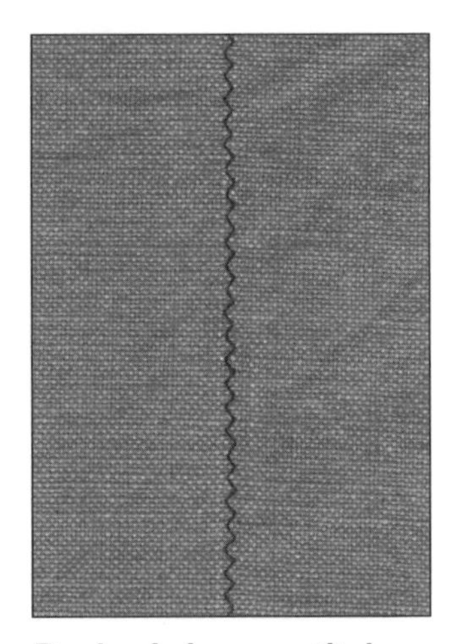

Back of zig-zag stitch

Supplies

FABRIC, PRE-WASHED

We pre-wash all our fabric in hot water and dry it in a hot dryer. This accomplishes several objectives — it shrinks the fabric as much as it will ever shrink, removes excess dye, and also removes the sizing.

Pre-washing is especially important for this method of appliqué because we recommend completely immersing or even washing the completed appliqué to remove the glue and make it possible to easily remove the freezer paper. If your fabric is going to shrink or the colors are going to run, you definitely want them to do so before you have completed your appliqué, not after! Removing the sizing makes the fabric softer so it's easier to turn under the edges of the appliqué pieces.

Some fabrics, especially reds, yellows and greens, can continue to bleed even after they have been washed once. Test these for further bleeding by washing them with a white cloth. If a fabric shows signs of unstable color, it is best to leave it out of your quilt.

Fabric choice. Sometimes fabric choice can make the appliqué easier. If you are working on a small shape with sharp points or narrow inside curves, choose thin, tightly woven fabric that won't ravel too much. Appliqué pieces cut from coarse fabrics fray and are hard to glue. Choose full-bodied fabric for backgrounds because they feed through the sewing machine more easily than thin fabrics.

FREEZER PAPER

We cut appliqué shapes from freezer paper — originally a kitchen staple. Freezer paper is packaged on a roll like aluminum foil and is available in the paper or canning/freezing sections of most grocery and discount stores. It's a white paper coated on one side with a thin layer of plastic. We refer to the coated side as the "shiny" side. Place the shiny side of the appliqué shape on the back of the appliqué fabric and iron it in place. The heat of the iron melts the plastic, adhering the piece to the fabric. Usually the paper can be lifted off and re-ironed several times. You can change your fabric choice several times using the same paper.

TRACING PENCIL OR PEN

To make your design look exactly as it is drawn, you will need to trace it on the shiny side of the freezer paper. Use a permanent fine-tipped felt pen. Other pens tend to smear and may leave marks on the fabric.

When you are working on symmetrical shapes, you can trace on either side of the paper. Then you can use a fine-point pencil to trace on the dull side of the paper.

SEAM RIPPER OR STILETTO

Choose a tool with a sharp tip. You will need it for smoothing the edges of the appliqué pieces. Wooden skewers also work well for turning the edges of the appliqué.

GLUE STICK

Use a white glue stick to adhere the seam allowance to the uncoated side of the freezer paper. A soft creamy glue stick like UHU, works best and doesn't have much smell.

We've tried fabric glue and rubber cement and think that UHU glue works better than either. Since we wash our quilt tops thoroughly, we 're not worried about glue residue.

CLEAN-UP TIPS

- **To keep your work-space clean while you use the glue stick, work on a plastic placemat or other item that can be washed with water. The washable glue will wipe off easily. Or, use a sheet of freezer paper as a disposable placemat.**
- **Keep a wet paper towel nearby to wipe your hands while you use the glue stick.**

ROXANNE'S GLU-BASTE IT,

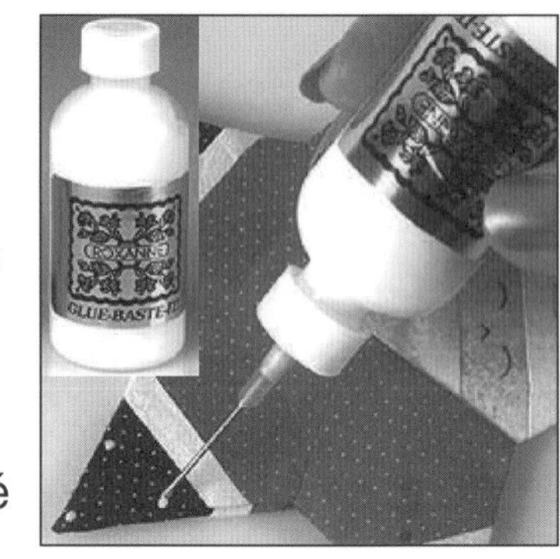

This is a thin, white glue packaged in a plastic bottle with a separate applicator tip. It is wonderful for basting the appliqué pieces in place on the background fabric. Before we discovered Roxanne's we used basting pins, which sometimes allowed the appliqué pieces to shift slightly as we sewed.

BIAS TAPE MAKERS

Although there are many ways to make bias strips, those made with bias-tape makers are the best for machine appliqué. Several companies manufacture tools in 1/4", 1/2", 3/4", 1" widths and larger sizes. Clover also makes a 3/8" tool, which we especially like. For more details, see page 16.

SCISSORS

You will need small, sharp scissors for cutting paper and fabric. The scissors should have 4" or 5" blades, fit well in your hand, and make a clean cut all the way to the tip of the blades. You don't need an expensive pair of scissors. You can buy a pair of Fiskars Micro-Tip scissors for less than $10, use them to cut both paper and fabric, and replace them with a new pair when they become too dull for fabric. Keep the old pair to use on paper only.

REMOVABLE OFFICE DOTS & CIRCLE TEMPLATES

To make perfect small circles, we use white, removable office dots, available in many office supply stores. These come in 1/2", 3/4" and 1" sizes and save time over cutting out circles from freezer paper. Be sure to buy white, removable dots. The colored ones may bleed onto your fabric, and the ones not labeled "removable" really are difficult to remove from the fabric.

When we need circles in other sizes, we often draw them using a plastic circle template instead of tracing them from the pattern. It's easier and more accurate to use the template if you have one. They are available at many office supply and discount stores.

Freezer Paper Basics

PREPARING THE APPLIQUÉ SHAPES

The most accurate way to prepare the appliqué shapes is to cut them out of freezer paper — one freezer-paper template for every appliqué shape in the quilt. Iron the template on the back of the appliqué fabric, cut out the fabric with a scant 1/4" seam allowance, and use a glue stick to adhere the seam allowance to the back of the freezer paper. If you cut an accurate freezer-paper piece and glue the edges under smoothly, the result will be a fabric shape with beautifully turned edges all ready to appliqué.

Of course, at some point you have to take that freezer paper out of your quilt, preferably before you quilt it! We talk about that on page 15.

First, some basics about preparing the appliqué:

CUTTING OUT THE FREEZER PAPER

Many appliqué designs and shapes are asymmetrical, meaning they face a certain direction. To make your appliquéd block match an asymmetrical pattern, trace the design pieces on the shiny side of the freezer paper. Use a permanent fine-tipped marker, because it will mark smoothly and will not smear easily. When you cut out the shape, cut just inside the marked line so no marker is left on the freezer paper. There are two reasons for this:

- When you fold the fabric edge over the freezer paper, you will be adding just a thread or two to the size of the appliqué piece. By cutting away the tracing line, you compensate for the amount of "growth" added by the fabric foldover.
- If you cut away the marker line, there is no chance that marker residue will rub off on your quilt fabric.

Symmetrical shapes. If your shape is symmetrical — exactly the same on each side if you fold it in half — you can trace on the uncoated side of the paper, which is a little easier. For example, the cactus plant in Lesson 1 is asymmetrical, so its pieces must be traced on the shiny side of the freezer paper. But its pot is symmetrical, so you could trace it on the uncoated side of the paper.

Cutting multiple pieces. You can cut up to four copies of the same shape at once. Trace the shape once. Place the traced sheet of freezer paper on top of three more sheets of freezer paper, all shiny-side up. Use the tip of your iron — steam off! — to tack the sheets of freezer paper together. You can do this by touching the tip of the iron to the stack of freezer paper for one or two seconds. Tack each shape at several intervals, being careful not to tack too close to the edge of the piece. The freezer-paper coatings will melt slightly, making the four sheets stick together. If your freezer paper stack isn't tacked together after one or two seconds, hold the iron tip at each place for another second or two. You will learn what works for your iron. Cut the shapes out, then carefully peel the four pieces apart.

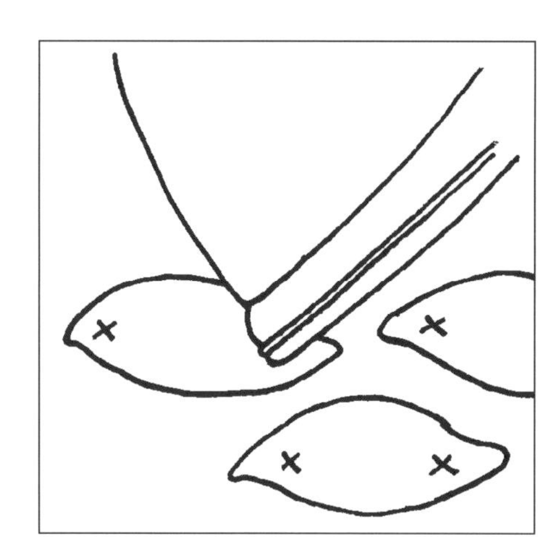

Cutting without tracing. If you have access to a photocopy machine, you can copy the pattern from the book. Please note that you have our permission to do so for your own personal use. See copyright notes, page 2.

Cut one to four sheets of freezer paper the same size as the photocopied image. Stack the sheets of freezer paper shiny-side up. Place the photocopied page on top of them, also facing up. Use an iron to tack the sheets together in several spots inside each appliqué shape. Cut out the appliqué pieces..

This method wastes some freezer paper because the shapes are not drawn closely together, but the paper is so inexpensive that the waste may not be an issue for you.

If the block has multi-layered designs such as flowers with centers, you will need to trace the extra design layers separately.

Cutting reverse-image shapes. These pieces, usually leaves, will be marked with a letter followed by (r) on the pattern shape. That means you should cut out one shape as it is drawn and a second copy that is just the reverse, or mirror-image, of the first. Our first examples are the sets of reversed leaves in Lesson 3.

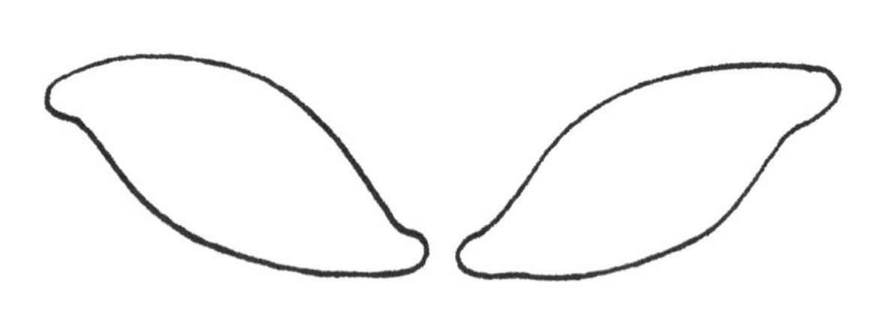

To cut reversed pieces, trace the shape once. Then place it, shiny sides together, with a second piece of freezer paper. Use the tip of a hot iron to tack the pieces together, then cut out both pieces at once.

Since you can cut four freezer-paper shapes at the same time, you can cut any combination of regular and reversed shapes at once. For two regular and two reversed shapes, place two sheets of freezer paper that are shiny side down on top of two sheets that are shiny side up. For one regular shape and three reversed, place three sheets of freezer paper shiny side down on top of one sheet that is shiny side up.

Ironing the freezer paper on the fabric. Place the freezer paper shapes on the wrong side of the fabric, leaving 1/2" between pieces to allow for seam allowance. If you accidentally position pieces too closely together, simply remove and reposition them.

Bias edges stretch more easily than straight edges, so try to place curved edges on the bias.

Cut out the fabric pieces with a scant 1/4" seam allowance.

Gluing. Place the appliqué shape paper-side-up on a work surface and apply the glue stick on the seam allowance. With a sharp tool or your fingers, fold the seam allowance over the paper, smoothing as you go. See the Sampler Lessons for more specific information about gluing various shapes.

TAKING OUT THE FREEZER PAPER

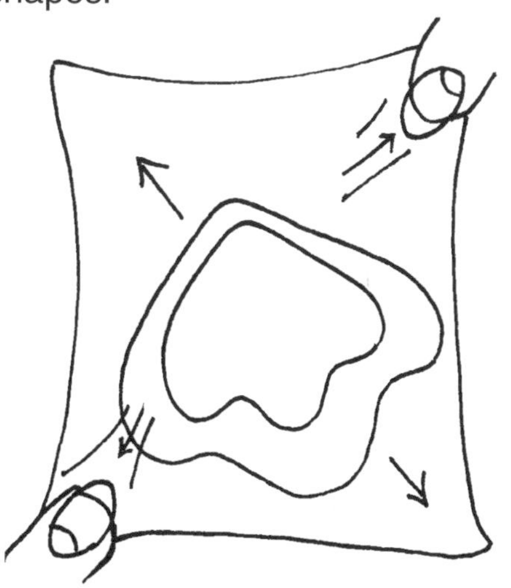

Whenever possible, start a block or quilt top with an oversized background. After all the stitching is complete, wash the block in cold water, gentle cycle, in your washing machine. This gets all the glue out of your quilt and releases the freezer paper's adherence to the back of the fabric. Dry it in the dryer with a clean dry towel to speed up the process.

When you take the block out of the dryer, resist the urge to iron it! Instead, use a pair of sharp-tipped scissors to cut out the background of the appliqué shapes, leaving a full 1/4" seam allowance around each piece.

If your stitching is narrow, you will be able to pull the paper out easily. If your stitching is a little wider, you may have to gently tug the background fabric around the shapes on the bias to release the paper.

Making bias vines

There are several ways to make bias vines for appliqué, but the method that works best for machine appliqué is to use a bias-tape maker. These come in a variety of sizes that are useful for everything from 1/4" stems to 1-1/2" or 2" border vines. In this book, we have used 1/4", 3/8" and 1/2" bias vines.

To make a length of bias tape,

- Cut a bias strip twice as wide as the desired finished size. If you need to seam together strips to make a longer length than you can cut from your yardage, sew the seams diagonally to spread out the bulk of the seam allowance.

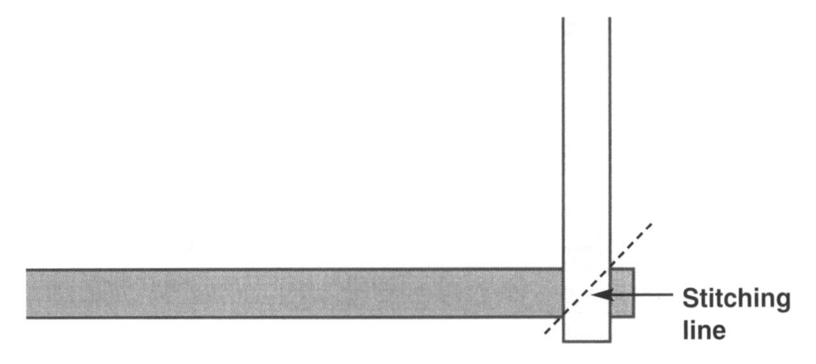

To sew a diagonal seam, place the ends of the strips right sides together with the top strip perpendicular to the bottom strip as shown above.

Sew a diagonal seam from the point where the strips cross at the bottom left to the point where they cross at the top right. Check to be sure the strip opens correctly, then trim and press the seam allowance to one side.

- Clip one end of the strip at an angle and spray it lightly with spray starch.
- Feed the angled end, right side of the fabric down, into the end of the bias-tape maker. Pin the tip of the strip to the ironing board.
- Pull the bias-tape maker along the bias strip, following just behind it with a hot iron. Pull carefully so you won't stretch the bias strip. The tape maker will fold under both edges and the hot iron will press them in place.
- Allow the tape to cool for a few minutes, then place it in your block or border.

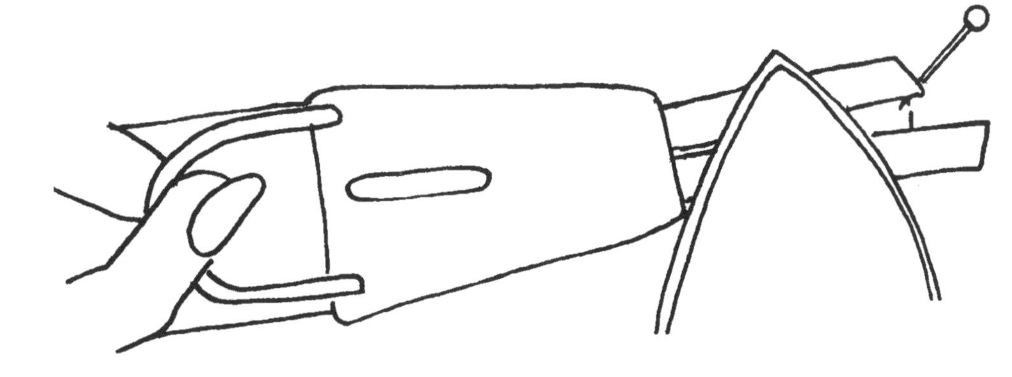

Making non-standard sizes. You can make your own homegrown bias-tape maker using just a couple of pins and your ironing board top. Place the first pin into the ironing board cover, leaving a space equal to the finished size of the bias tape under the pin. Place a second pin about an inch away, parallel to the first pin and also with a space underneath that is equal to the finished size of the bias strip. Cut the fabric strip twice the finished size of the vine. Fold under both edges and press with a hot iron. Carefully feed the strip through the set of pins, following with an iron to press the edges in place.

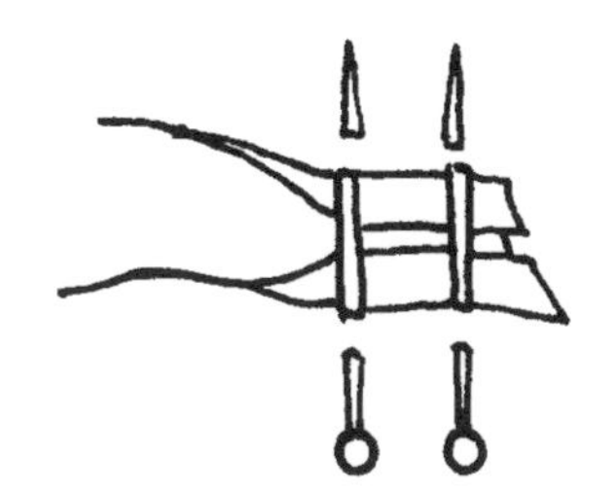

Saving unused bias tape. If you won't be using the bias vine immediately, wrap it around a cardboard tube to keep it in shape. We save all our extra bias this way. When we're making a new block and need just a few 1/4" stems, we check our bias vine "stash" to see if we have something already made that will work!

Why not other methods? There are several other ways to make bias vines, but they are not as easy to use as the bias tape.

Many quiltmakers make bias vines by sewing a bias tube and ironing it over a heat-proof bar to place the seam at the back of the tube. But we found that the tube's seam created a hump down the center of the vine. The hump was unsightly, and it interfered with the edge of the presser foot as we tried to sew the vine. The bias tape method uses less fabric and produces a flatter piece.

Another way to create a bias vine is to fold a bias strip in half, right sides out, and place the raw edges along the design area of the quilt. Sew the bias strip to the quilt with a 1/4" seam allowance, then flip the folded edge of the strip over and and appliqué it in place. This method encases the seam allowance inside the vine, and needs to be appliquéd on only one side. But it is difficult to precisely place the bias strip on the quilt. The bias tape makers use less fabric and the result is a vine that you can place exactly on the background fabric.

Sampler Quilt Lessons

Make the blocks in lessons 1-9 and add a border from lesson 10 or 11 to learn how to successfully appliqué a variety of designs.

NEW CENTURY GARDEN

65" square sampler
15" blocks • 10-1/2" finished appliqué border

FABRIC REQUIREMENTS

Dark brown for background of five blocks: 1-1/2 yards
Medium brown for background of four blocks and bias vine in border: 1-1/2 yards.
Pumpkin for background of border: 2 yards
Quarter yards of the following colors for appliqué:

- 3 greens
- 2 reds
- 3 golds, at least one plaid
- 2 oranges, at least one plaid
- 1 light violet/blue
- 1 medium violet
- 1 black floral
- 2 light prints

BACKGROUND CUTTING INSTRUCTIONS

- From the dark brown fabric, cut five 16-1/2" squares. These will be used for the blocks in Lessons 1, 3, 5, 7 and 9. Save the remainder for appliqué pieces in the border.
- From the medium brown fabric, cut four 16-1/2" squares for the blocks in Lessons 2, 4, 6 and 8. Also cut enough 1" bias strips to make nine 1" x 30" bias strips. To use the fabric efficiently, arrange the squares and bias strips as shown at right. There is not quite enough room to cut the bias strips on an exact 45° angle. Don't worry; the angle is close enough.

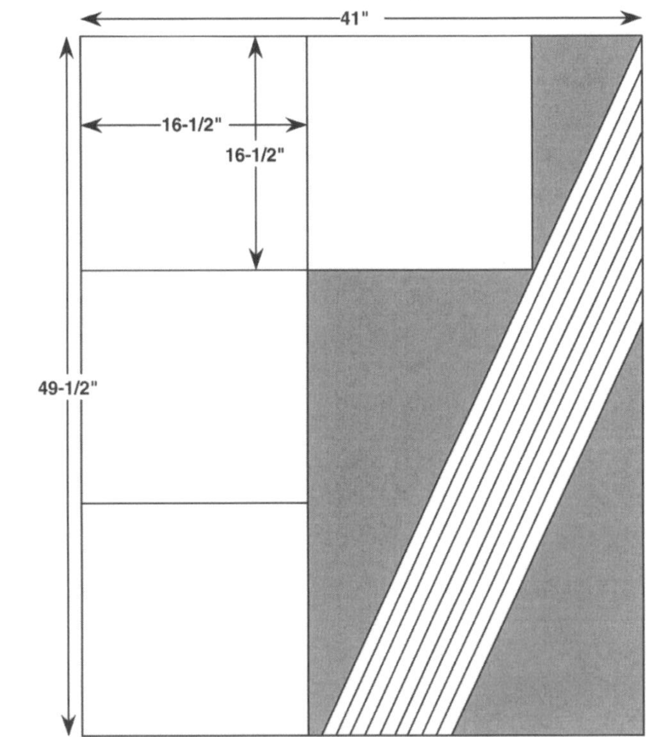

NEW CENTURY SAMPLER

50" square sampler
15" blocks • 2-1/2" finished dogtooth border

FABRIC REQUIREMENTS

Light fabric for background of five blocks and border: 2 yards
Light fabric for background of four blocks: 4 fat quarters
Red for sawtooth border: 1/2 yard
Quarter yards of the following colors for appliqué:

- 2 yellows
- 2 reds
- 2 blacks
- 2 oranges, one plaid
- 1 medium blue
- 1 tan floral
- 1 navy floral

BACKGROUND CUTTING INSTRUCTIONS

- From each of the four light fat quarters, cut one 16-1/2" square. These are for the blocks in Lessons 2, 4, 6 and 8.
- From the 2 yards of light fabric, cut five 16-1/2" squares, two 3" x 50-1/2" strips and two 3" x 45-1/2" strips as shown at right.

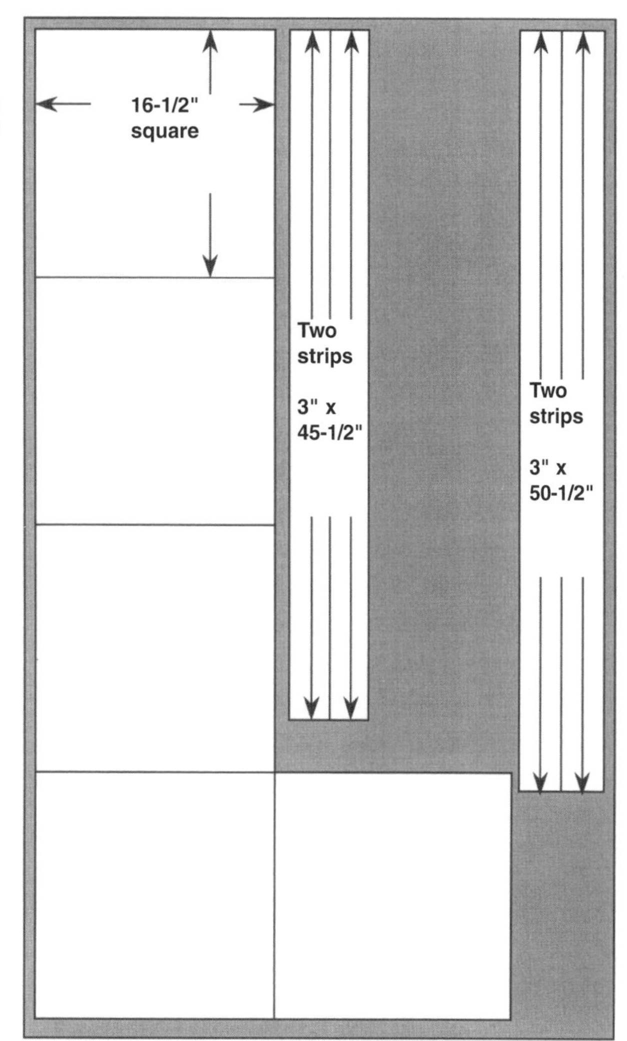

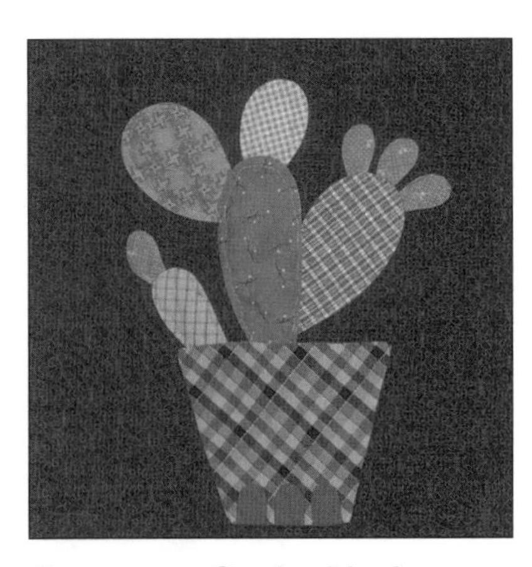

***Damascus Garden* block.** *Damascus* was a machine sold by Montgomery Ward and Company.

Lesson 1 — Outer Curves, Layering

FABRIC REQUIREMENTS FOR THE *DAMASCUS GARDEN* BLOCK

- **Background fabric:** 16-1/2" square, cut oversized to be trimmed to 15-1/2" after appliqué is complete
- **Flower pot:** 8"
- **Cactus:** 3" x 8" for large bract, 4 " x 6" for 3 small ones, 5 fabrics in all
- **Cactus blooms**: 5" square

PREPARING THE FREEZER PAPER

You will need one freezer-paper template for each pattern piece. The pot is symmetrical; you can trace it on the dull side of the freezer paper if you wish. Everything else is asymmetrical and should be traced on the shiny side of the freezer paper.

CUTTING AND CLIPPING

Iron each freezer paper template onto the back of the fabric you have chosen for that piece. Cut out each with a scant 1/4" seam allowance. Mark the bottom of each piece where it will tuck under another part of the cactus or pot. You can leave a little extra seam allowance in these tuck-under areas.

Since this block has only outer curves, it requires no clipping. Clipping is reserved for inner points and curves only.

TURNING UNDER THE SEAM ALLOWANCES

Turn under the outer edges of each piece, leaving raw edges where a piece will be tucked under another. On this block, only the flower pot and its decorative tongues will be glued all the way around. All the other pieces have a raw edge that will be tucked under another piece.

Run the glue stick around the outer edge of the freezer-paper shape. Use a light touch, taking care not to pull the fabric edge away from the freezer paper. At the flower-pot corners and the rounded edges of the cactus bracts, put extra glue on the fabric edge as well as the paper edge.

Use a sharp-pointed utensil such as a stiletto or seam ripper to fold the seam allowance to the back of the pattern piece. As you turn under the edge with one hand, follow along with the forefinger of your other hand to press the seam allowance in place.

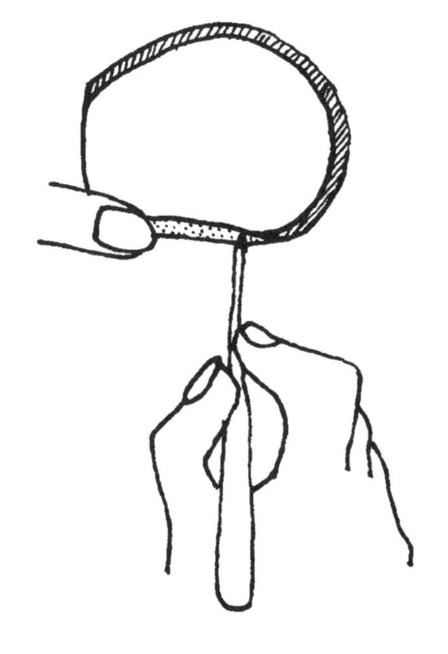

The flat edges and gentle curves will fold over smoothly.

When you get to the more pronounced curves at the pot corners and the tops of the cactus bracts, use the tip of the stiletto to form narrow pleats in the seam allowance as you fold it over the edge of the freezer paper. The folded edge will look as if it has been gathered around the curve.

When you've turned the entire seam, examine the front. If you find any rough edges, turn the piece over and use the stiletto to smooth out the imperfections while the glue is still wet.

The flower pot tongues have square edges at the bottom. First, glue the sides and outer curve of each tongue. Then glue the bottom edge and fold it up.

Cherie's fabric gluing tip: If using a sharp-pointed tool is awkward for you, pick up the appliqué piece in one hand and try using the thumb of your other hand to turn under the seam allowance. When you've turned the entire seam, examine the front. If you find any rough edges, turn the piece over and use a sharp-pointed tool on the back to smooth out the imperfections.

This method works well for people with small, dexterous hands.

LAYERED DESIGNS

Working with designs that have layered parts, such as the decorative tongues at the bottom of the flower pot, is a little tricky. If you position all the pieces on the background fabric and then sew the tongues in place, you would be appliquéing the pieces to two layers of fabric. In general, it is best to avoid appliquéing to more than one layer of fabric because of the problems it causes in cutting out the background and removing the freezer paper. See Lesson 3 for an illustration of this problem.

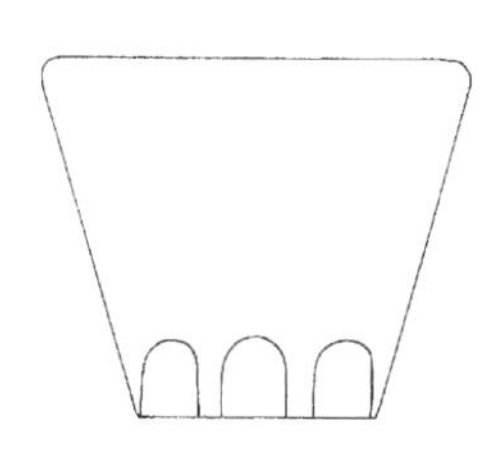

In this case, the easiest way to deal with the two-layer basket is to appliqué the flower pot first, cut out the background behind it, then appliqué the tongues in place.

PATTERN PLACEMENT

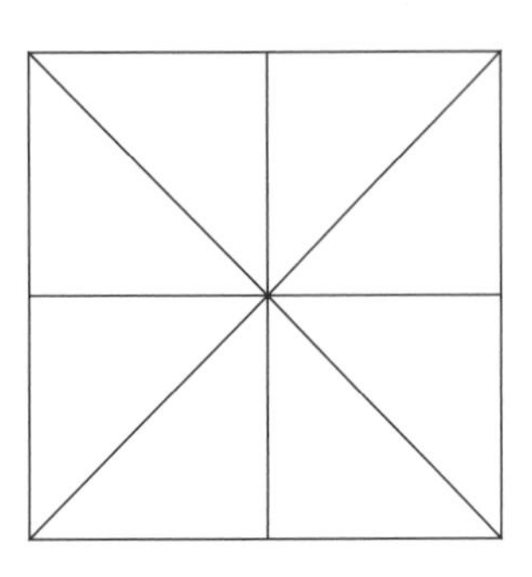

There's no need to trace the design on your back ground fabric or to use a light table. This is an easy block to arrange.

First, fold the background square in half horizontally, vertically and diagonally in both directions, pressing the center line at each fold. When you unfold the block, you will have pressed lines to mark the horizontal and vertical center of the block as well as the diagonal center lines.

Lay the background fabric on a flat surface. Lightly fold the flower pot in half vertically to find its center top and center bottom points.

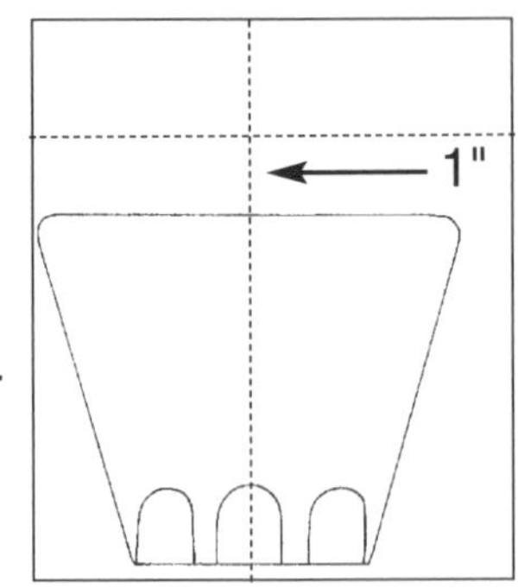

Line up the center of the flower pot with the vertical center of the background fabric, placing the flower pot 1" below the horizontal center of the block.

Refer to the pattern to place the rest of the pieces. By looking at each shape's position in reference to the center vertical and horizontal lines, you can place them accurately.

BASTING

Use the Roxanne's Glu-Baste-It to hold the pieces in place. Run the bottle's applicator tip just under the edge of each piece to place a thin thread of glue. Press down the edges with your fingers and allow the glue to dry. The Glu-Baste-It will hold the appliqué pieces securely in place while you sew. No pins!

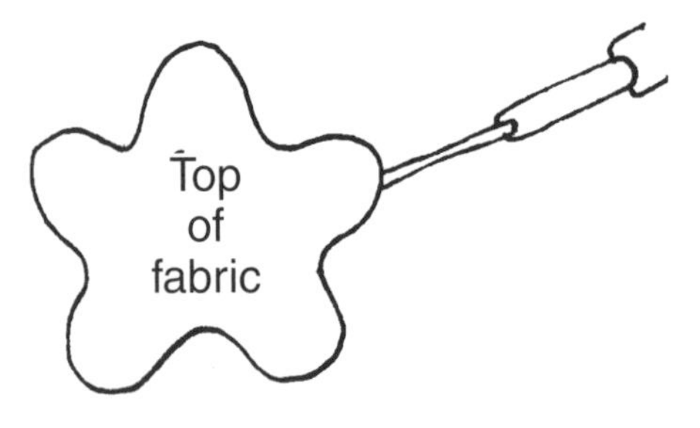

Put the applicator tip of the Roxanne's glue bottle under the edge of each appliqué piece to place a thin thread of basting glue.

SEWING

First sew around the flower pot. Cut out the background behind the flower pot, then glue down the decorative tongues and sew around each of them.

When you sew the entire way around a shape, you can secure the beginning and ending stitches by sewing the last few stitches over the first few stitches.

When you sew the cactus bracts, you will be sewing only partially around each shape. Use stay-stitching to secure the beginning and ending stitches. Start sewing at the point where the cactus tucks under another piece. Stay stitch by holding the fabric in place under the machine needle while you take five or six stitches. Stay-stitch again when you finish sewing around each piece.

LESSONS FOR ADAPTING OTHER DESIGNS

By making each cactus bract a separate piece, we avoided putting inside corners in this design. If the cactus had been cut from one piece, we would have had to clip the seam allowance at each inside corner to allow the fabric to spread apart at the corner. Every clipped point creates a "raw edge" that weakens the appliqué and must be carefully stitched to be stabilized.

If your next appliqué project has a vine and leaves cut from the same piece of fabric, consider redrafting the design to make the leaves separate pieces that would tuck under the vine instead.

To turn under the seam allowance on an inside point, you must clip first. The clipped point will have only a thread or two that can be turned under.

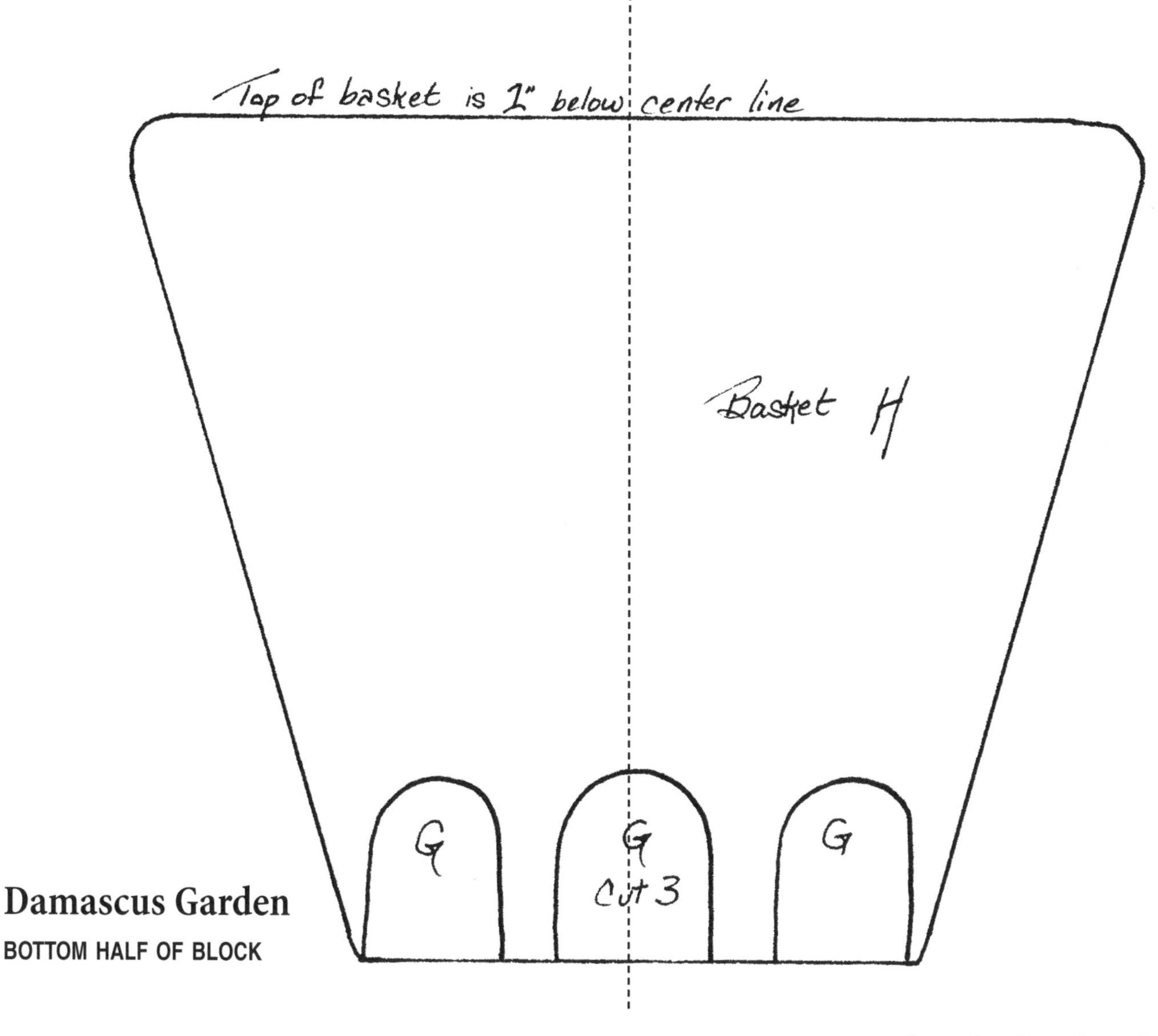

Damascus Garden

BOTTOM HALF OF BLOCK

Damascus Garden

TOP OF CACTUS POT

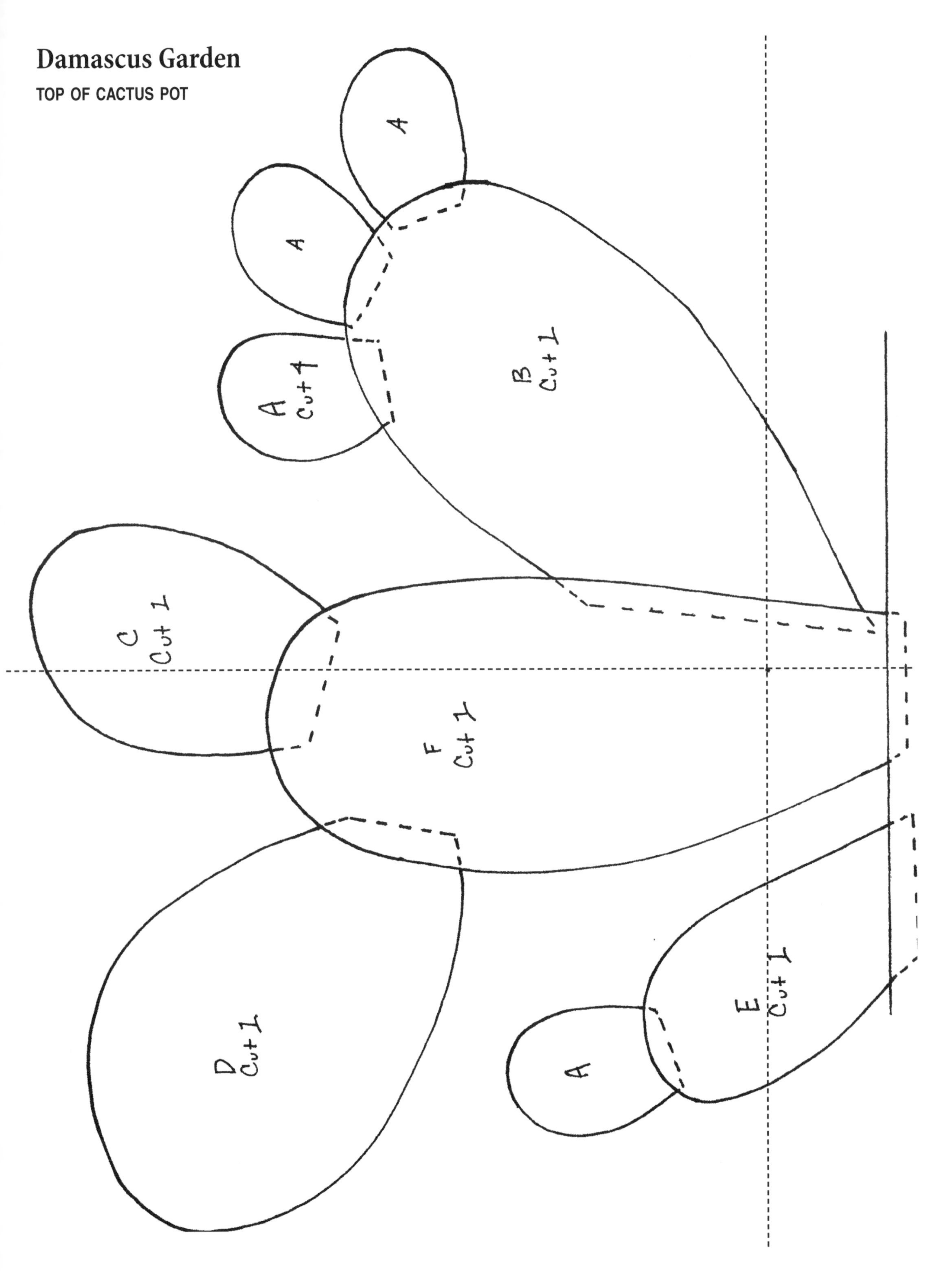

Lesson 2 — Bias Strips, Inner Angles, Outer Points

***New Home Wreath* block.** *New Home* advertised with a variety of colored trade cards at the end of the 19th century.

FABRIC REQUIREMENTS FOR *NEW HOME WREATH* BLOCK

- **Background fabric:** 16-1/2" square, cut oversized to be trimmed to 15-1/2" after appliqué is complete
- **Vine for wreath:** 6-1/2" x 13" rectangle
- **Leaves:** 6" x 10" rectangle
- **Stars:** 9" square

BIAS VINE FOR THE WREATH

The 1/2" bias vine is separated by the placement of the stars, so you will not need to make one continuous length of vine. Instead, make four strips of vine, each approximately 8" long. To make the vine, cut four 1" x 8" bias strips and clip one end of each on the diagonal. Feed each strip through a 1/2" bias-tape maker. See page 16 for more about bias vines.

PREPARING THE FREEZER PAPER

You will need one freezer-paper template for each of the other pattern pieces, but the good news is that all of them are symmetrical and you can cut more than one at a time. Trace one star and three leaves on either side of the freezer paper. Stack that piece of freezer paper on top of three others, all facing the same direction. Tack them together with a hot iron and cut them out as we have described on page 13.

CUTTING AND CLIPPING

Iron each freezer paper template onto the back of the fabric you have chosen for that piece. Cut out each with a scant 1/4" seam allowance. Make the seam allowances slightly narrower at the tips of the leaves and the star points.

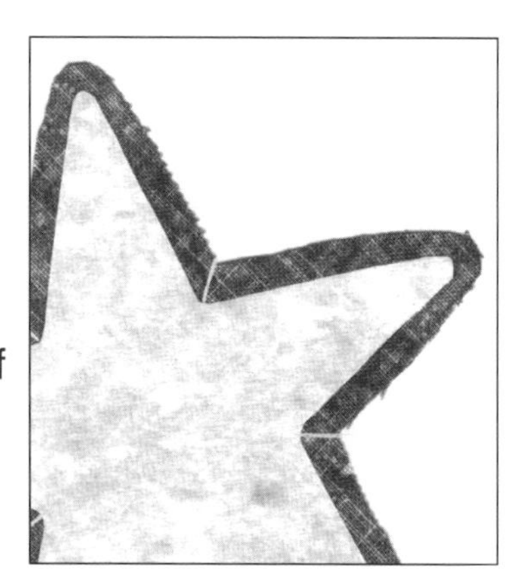

Make one clip at each inside angle of the stars. The clip should stop a thread or two from the edge of the freezer paper. If you clip into the freezer paper, the cut will be exposed on the top of the appliqué piece.

TURNING UNDER THE SEAM ALLOWANCES

The awful truth about sharp points. It's easy to make a sharp point, as long as the angle of the point is close to 90° (the angle of a square corner) or more. When the angles are that wide, you can turn under the seam allowance on one edge, then fold over the other edge with plenty of room for the folds to fit inside the angle.

When the angle is smaller than 90°, there is not as much room for the seam allowances to fit inside the angle. In those cases, it can be much more difficult to make a sharp point. Hand appliqué artists use a five-step folding and stitching method to make sharp tips. Machine appliqué artists can make a multi-step fold, but it often results in a thick point tip that flattens out under the weight of the presser foot.

We've drawn this pattern with easy-to-make points. Even though the leaf points are sharp, the wide angle of the point affords enough room to turn under the seam allowance without clipping or making multiple folds.

We've drawn the stars with blunt, curved points that you can gather or pinch around the edge. If you'd like to try sharp star points, follow the directions at the bottom of this page.

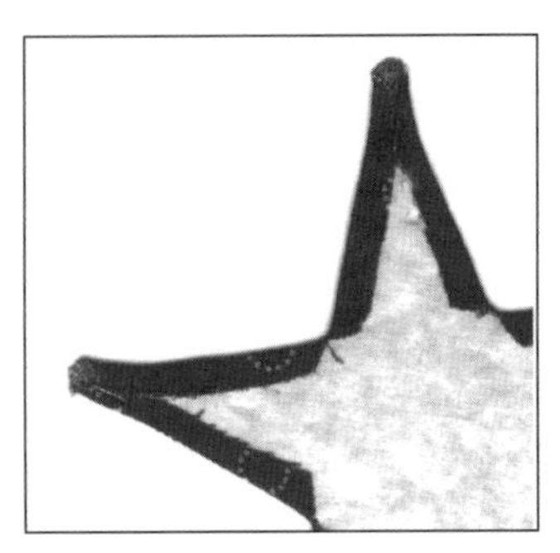

Cherie's star-folding tip: If using a sharp-pointed tool is awkward for you, use your fingers to turn under the seam allowances.

Work on one star point at a time. Start at the inner angles, folding both seam allowances over as you work toward the star tip.

When you are close to the tip, use your thumb and forefinger to pinch together the point where the seam allowances meet. While pinching the point, fold the extra seam allowance to the back of the star tip. Use a stiletto or other sharp tool to smooth out any rough edges.

Start with the leaves.

- Glue and turn under one edge of each leaf.
- Then glue and turn under the other edge.
- If the second seam allowance sticks out past the edge of the leaf after it is turned under, use the stiletto to nudge it into place under the tip.

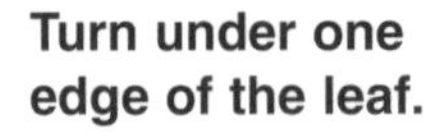

Turn under one edge of the leaf.

Turn under the other edge. The seam allowance will fit inside the tip.

To glue the rounded-edge stars, start at a clipped inside angle.

- Apply the glue stick to the paper and seam allowance of one tip, then use the stiletto to fold over one side.
- When you get to the outer tip, use the stiletto to make small pleats in the seam allowance as you fold over the edge.
- Continue folding the edge until you're at the next inside angle. Continue on to the next tip.

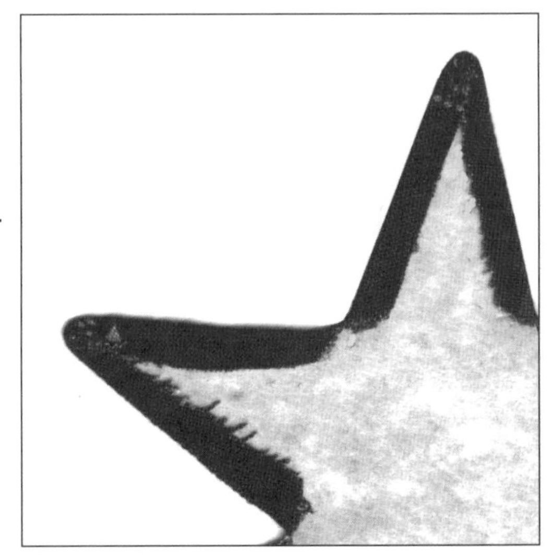

- Pay special attention to gluing the inside angle. There should be one or two threads in the seam allowance just at the clipped point. Put plenty of glue in that spot. Use the tip of your finger to firmly roll those threads over to the back of the freezer paper.

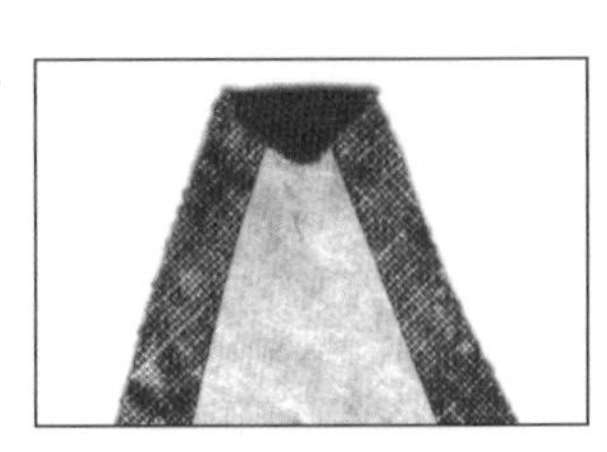

To make sharp star tips,

- Dab the glue stick at each point and turn under the top edge.
- Apply the glue stick to one side of each star point and turn it under.

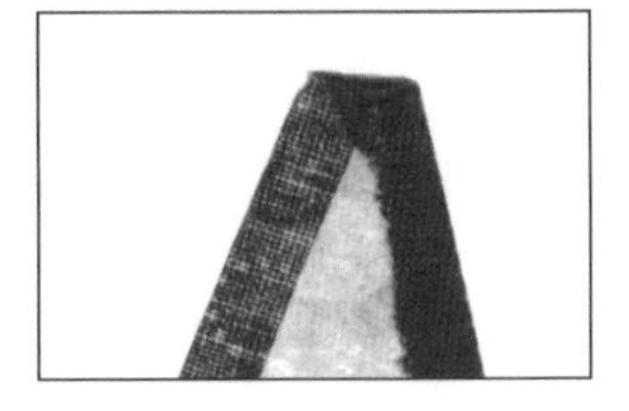

- Apply the glue stick to the other side of each star point and turn under that edge. If part of the seam allowance extends past the edge of the star, try using the stiletto to fold it back under the point.

  You can cut away the extra seam allowance, as long as you don't clip near the star point. We allow clipping at inner angles and curves because it is a necessary evil, but we try to avoid clipping outer points at all costs. Sometimes you can use your fingernails to pinch the folded point to a sharper shape.

If the seam allowance extends past the star's edge, try folding it back under the point.

PATTERN PLACEMENT

Press horizontal, vertical and diagonal guidelines in the background square as described in Lesson 1.

To help with pattern placement, make a placement template:

- Photocopy the pattern onto a heavy piece of paper or trace it onto the dull side of a piece of freezer paper. If you use freezer paper, place the freezer paper, shiny sides facing, with another piece of freezer paper and iron the two sheets together.
- Cut the stars, vine, and inside leaf away from the pattern as shown at right. This creates a "negative-space" placement template for one quarter of the block.

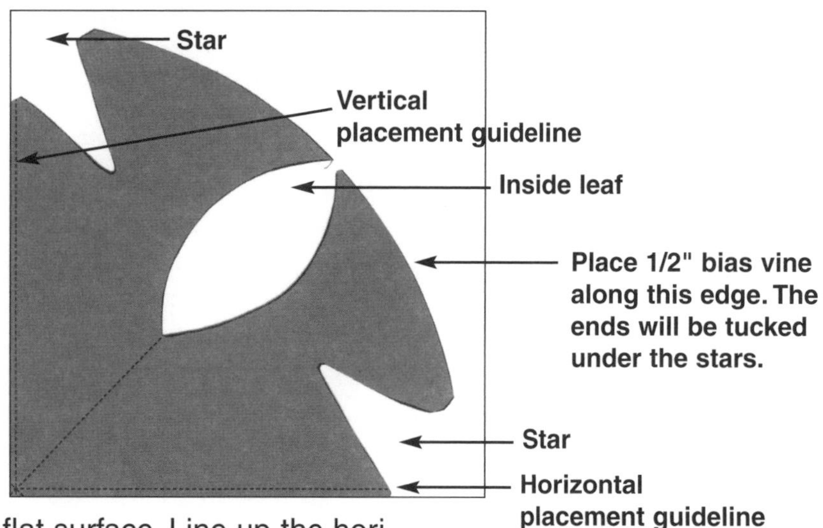

- Lay the background fabric on a flat surface. Line up the horizontal, vertical, and diagonal guidelines of the template with the corresponding lines on the background fabric.
- The inside edge of the bias vine should be placed right along the curve of the template, with each end tucked under a star. Place a thin line of Roxanne's Glu-Baste-It beside the curved edge of the paper, and place the bias vine. Place the inner curve smoothly and let the outer curve stretch to fit into place.
- Next place one star and the inside leaf. Run a thin line of glue under the edges and press them into place.
- Move the placement template to an adjoining quarter of the background fabric and place another bias vine, leaf and star. Move clockwise or counterclockwise around the block until you have placed all the vines, stars and inner leaves.
- Place the outer leaves at an angle on either side of the block's diagonal lines, with their points just touching the outside curve of the bias vine. Refer to the pattern for placement. Use the Roxanne's glue to baste them to the background.

SEWING

First sew both sides of the bias vine. Be sure to tuck the ends of the vine under the stars. You can hide your beginning and ending vine stitches under the edges of the stars. Or, stay stitch by holding the fabric in place under the machine needle while you take five or six stitches at the beginning and end of each vine.

Next, sew around the stars and the leaves. Stay stitch at the inner angles of the stars, where the clipping has left just a thread to be turned under as seam allowance. The extra stitching will help secure the nearly raw edge of the inner angle. Secure the beginning and ending stitches by sewing the last few stitches over the first few stitches.

If you chose to appliqué stars with sharp points, take special care at the tips. The glued tip will be thick because you have folded three thicknesses of seam allowance under it. The weight and motion of the presser foot tends to flatten out the tip, blunting the point. To keep the point sharp, use the stiletto to hold one side of the tip in place as you sew the other side.

LESSONS FOR ADAPTING OTHER DESIGNS

We made our star points slightly rounded to make it easier to turn under the seam allowance. The rounded points need no clipping to make the seam allowance fit under the point, so they are more stable than sharp points with narrower seam allowances.

If you fall in love with a pattern that has narrow, sharp points, consider whether it would look just as good with narrow, rounded points. Feel free to round the tips of the points if that will help you produce a beautifully sewn quilt. It's your quilt; you can change the pattern whenever you wish!

New Home Wreath

ONE QUARTER OF THE WREATH DESIGN

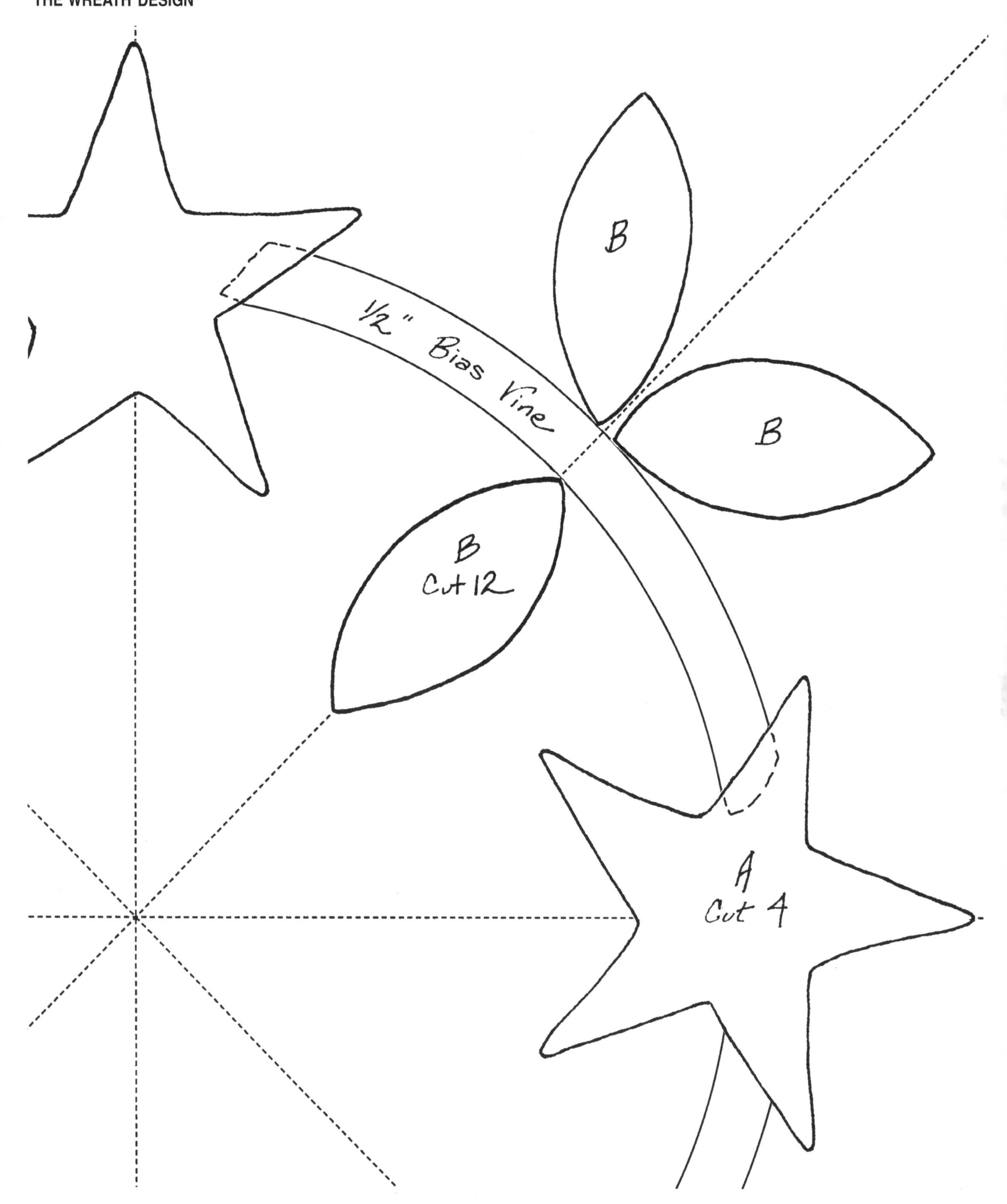

***Domestic Garden* block.** *Domestic* machines evoked cozy images of the contented homemaker as did machines with names such as *Household* and *Family.*

Lesson 3 — Inner Curves, Outer Curves, Reversing Pattern Shapes

FABRIC REQUIREMENTS FOR THE *DOMESTIC GARDEN* BLOCK

- **Background fabric:** 16-1/2" square, cut oversized to be trimmed to 15-1/2" after appliqué is complete
- **Flower pot:** 6" x 8-1/2" rectangle. If you are using striped or other directional fabric, you may need extra fabric.
- **Flower pot border:** 2" x 8-1/2"
- **Large flowers:** 4-1/2" x 13" rectangle
- **Flower centers:** 2-1/2" x 7-1/2" rectangle
- **Leaves & stems:** 6-1/2" squares of two different fabrics

PREPARING THE FREEZER PAPER

You will need one freezer-paper template for each pattern piece. The pot, flowers and flower centers are symmetrical; you can trace them on the dull side of the freezer paper if you wish. Use the directions on page 13 to cut the three flowers and flower centers at once. You will need to cut two of each leaf shape, one the reverse image of the other. See page 14 for instructions. Don't make freezer-paper templates for the stems; we recommend making 1/2" bias vine instead.

CUTTING AND CLIPPING

To make the stems, cut a 1" bias strip from corner to opposite diagonal corner of each 6-1/2" square. Cut one end at a diagonal and feed them through a 1/2" bias tape maker. See page 16 for more detailed instructions. You will need a 6" length for the main stem and 3" and 3-1/2" lengths for the two side stems.

For the other shapes, iron each freezer paper template onto the back of the fabric you have chosen for that piece. Cut out each with a scant 1/4" seam allowance. At the top of the flower pot, you can leave a little extra seam allowance where the top will tuck under the flower pot border.

Don't clip any of the outer curves. On the inner curves, make just one clip to the center of the curve. The clip should stop a thread or two from the edge of the freezer paper. If you clip into the freezer paper, the cut will be exposed on the top of the appliqué piece.

TURNING UNDER THE SEAM ALLOWANCES

Turn under the outer edges of each piece, leaving raw edges where a piece will be tucked under another. On this block, the flower pot border, flowers and flower centers will be glued all the way around. All the other pieces have a raw edge that will be tucked under another piece.

Run the glue stick around the outer edge of the freezer-paper shape. Use a light touch, taking care not to pull the fabric edge away from the freezer paper. At the rounded edges, put extra glue on the fabric edge as well as the paper edge.

Use a sharp-pointed tool such as a stiletto or seam ripper to fold the seam allowance to the back of the pattern piece. As you turn under the edge with one hand, follow along with the forefinger of your other hand to press the seam allowance in place.

When you get to the more clipped curves on the flower pot border and the flowers, there should be one or two threads in the seam allowance just at the clipped points Put plenty of glue in that spot. Use the tip of your finger to firmly roll those threads over to the back of the freezer paper. Be sure to glue under even the smallest threads that may be turned to the back of the piece.

LAYERED DESIGNS

The flower centers should be sewn on top of the flowers before you position all the pieces on the background. If you placed all the pieces on the background before you sewed the flower centers in place, you would be appliquéing the centers to two layers of fabric, causing problems in cutting out the background and removing the freezer paper.

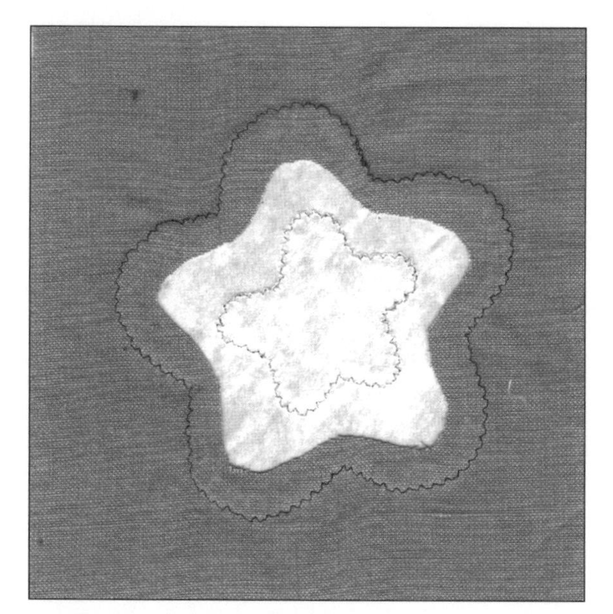

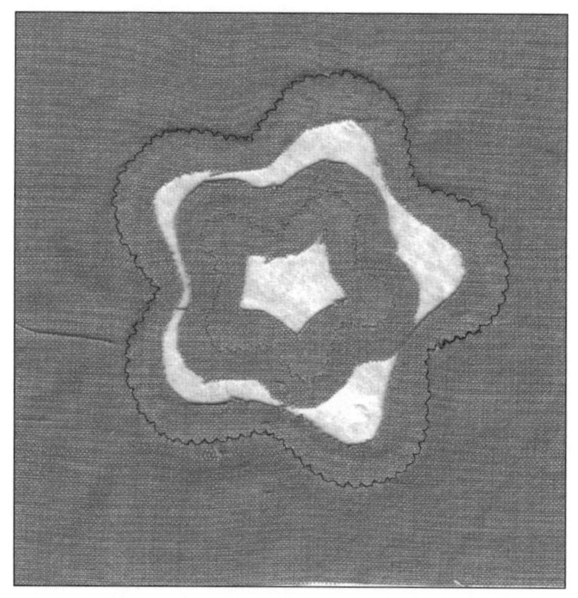

In the sample at left, the flower center was sewn to the flower before the flower was sewn to the background. This allows the quiltmaker to cut out the background behind the flower, take out the freezer paper, then cut out the background of the flower center.

In the sample at right, the flower center was sewn after the flower was placed on top of the the background fabric. Since the stitching goes through both layers, the quiltmaker cannot then cut out the entire background behind the flower.

PATTERN PLACEMENT AND BASTING

Like the first block, this block can be arranged by referring to the guidelines on the pattern.

Press horizontal, vertical and diagonal guidelines in the background square as instructed in Lesson 1.

Lay the background fabric on a flat surface. Glue the flower pot border to the top of the flower pot, then lightly fold them in half vertically to find the center top and bottom points. Line up the center of the flower pot with the vertical center of the background fabric, placing the top of the flower pot 1" below the horizontal center of the block.

Refer to the pattern to place the rest of the pieces. By looking at each shape's position in reference to the center vertical and horizontal lines, you can place them accurately. Tuck the leaves under the flower stems.

Use Roxanne's glue to baste the pieces in place.

SEWING

Treat the clipped edges of the inner curves the same way you did the inner angles in Lesson 2 — stay stitch at the clipped inner curve. The extra stitches will help stabilize the point where there is very little seam allowance at the inside clipping.

LESSONS FOR ADAPTING OTHER DESIGNS

The two-piece flowers in this block were not too difficult to prepare. But some designs have as many as four or five pieces stacked on top of each other. Just remember to work from the top down, no matter how many layers the design may have. Appliqué the top layer to the one under it. Then appliqué that two-layer set to the third piece in the design and keep going until you have assembled and sewn together the entire design to be appliquéd to the background block.

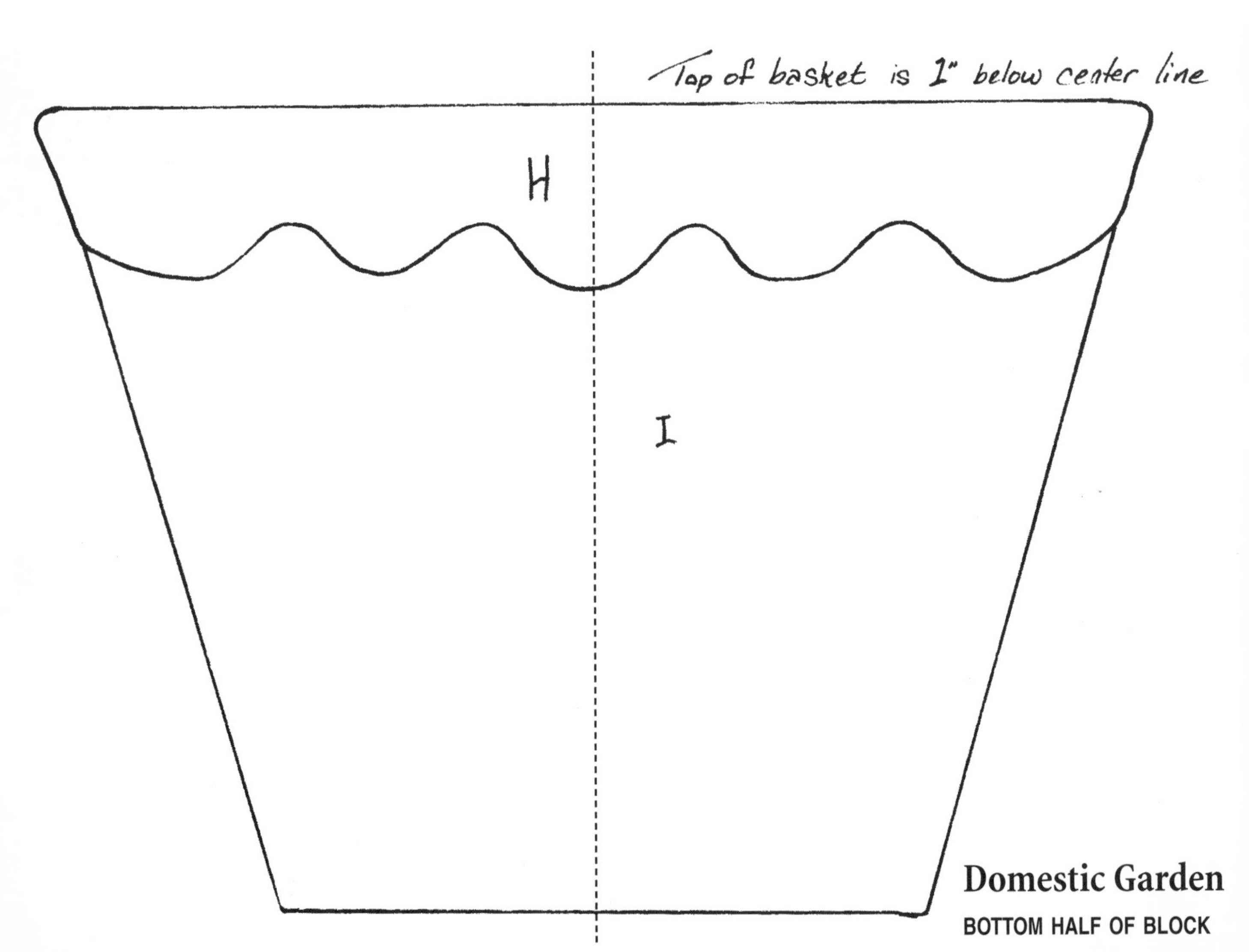

Domestic Garden

BOTTOM HALF OF BLOCK

Domestic Garden

TOP OF BLOCK

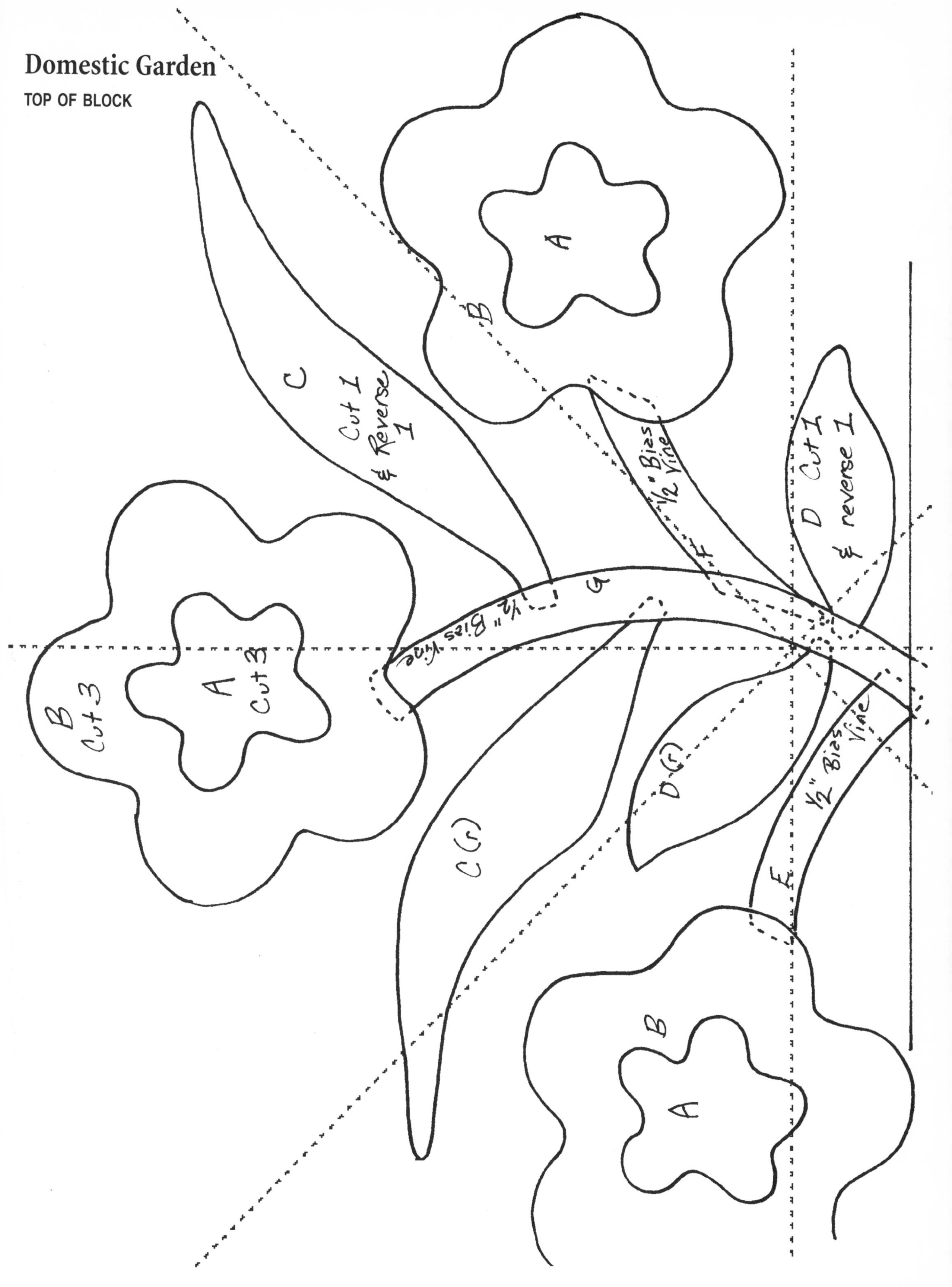

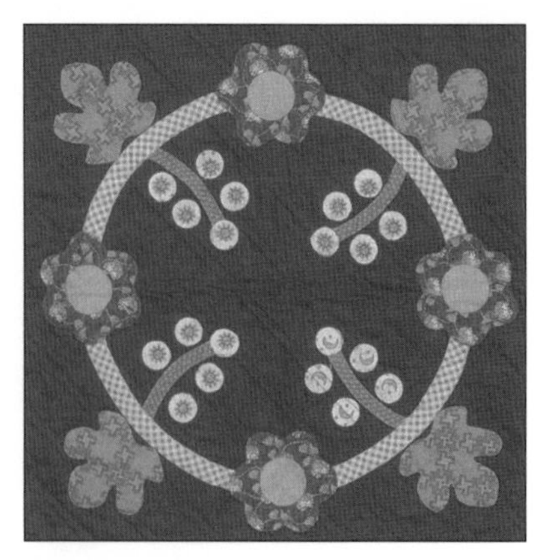

***Singer's Wreath* block.** Rather than invent the sewing machine, Isaac *Singer* was the first to manufacture a home machine, and the company popularized the installment plan to make machines affordable.

Lesson 4 — Narrow Inner Curves, Berries

FABRIC REQUIREMENTS FOR *SINGER'S WREATH* BLOCK

- **Background fabric:** 16-1/2" square, cut oversized to be trimmed to 15-1/2" after appliqué is complete
- **Vine for wreath:** 6-1/2" x 13" rectangle
- **Leaves:** 8" square
- **Flowers:** 8" square
- **Flower centers:** 5" square
- **Stems:** 9" square
- **Berries:** 9" square

PREPARING THE FREEZER PAPER

Instead of cutting freezer-paper templates for the wreath, make four 8" lengths of 1/2" bias vine. For the stems, make four 4" lengths of 1/4" bias vine. Directions are on page 35.

You will be able to make a smoother edge on the flower centers if you draw them with a plastic circle template, available at most office supply and discount stores. The flower centers are 1-1/4" circles. Make the circles from two layers of freezer paper. Trace 2 circles and layer the freezer paper with three other sheets to make multiple copies, as we describe on page 13. Instead of separating each set into four pieces, separate it into two pieces. You will be putting a lot of pressure on the circle edge as you glue, and the stiffer template will hold its edge better than a single-layer of freezer paper. It also will be easier to remove from the finished block.

If you have access to removable white office dots, use the 3/4" dots for the berry templates. The advantages to using the dots are that they are perfect circles, and you do not have to cut them out. If you need to cut the 3/4" circles from freezer paper, draw them with a circle template and cut them double-layered, like the flower centers.

The leaves and flowers are symmetrical and you can cut more than one at a time. Trace one of each and follow the directions on page 13 to cut out four at one time.

CUTTING AND CLIPPING

Iron each freezer paper template onto the back of the fabric you have chosen. Cut out each with a scant 1/4" seam allowance.

Make one clip at each inside curve of the flowers and at the wide curve at the bottom of the leaf.

The narrow, sharp inside curves at the top of leaf don't leave very much room for a seam allowance. To make the most of the small seam allowance, make a "Y" cut at these narrow inner curves as shown at left.

Stop clipping a thread or two from the edge of the freezer paper. If you clip into the freezer paper, the cut will be exposed on the top of the appliqué piece.

TURNING UNDER THE SEAM ALLOWANCES

Glue and turn under the outer edges of each piece. On this block, all the freezer paper shapes will be glued all the way around. Only the 1/4" bias stems will be tucked under another piece.

You will need to put extra glue on the seam allowances of the flower centers and berries. Use a stiletto to make small pleats in the seam allowance as you glue down the circles and sharp curves.

When you get to the clipped inner curves on the leaves, there should be just a thread or two of seam allowance at the clipped point. Put plenty of glue in that spot. Use the tip of your finger to firmly roll those threads over to the back of the freezer paper. Be sure to glue under even the smallest threads that may be turned to the back of the piece.

LAYERED DESIGNS

Sew the flower center on top of each flower first, before you position the pieces on the background. See Lesson 3 for more details about layered designs.

BIAS VINE FOR THE WREATH & STEMS

Make four strips of vine, each approximately 8" long. Cut four 1" x 8" bias strips and clip one end of each on the diagonal. Feed each strip through a 1/2" bias-tape maker.

For the stems, make four strips of 1/4" vine. Start with four 1/2" strips, each with one end cut on the diagonal. Feed them through a 1/4" bias tape maker. See page 16 for more about bias vines.

PATTERN PLACEMENT

Press horizontal, vertical and diagonal guidelines in the background square as instructed in Lesson 1.

To help with pattern placement, make and use a placement template like the one described in Lesson 2, page 27.

Flower

Vertical placement guideline

Place 1/2" bias vine along this edge. The ends will be tucked under the flowers

1/4" bias stem

Berry

Flower

Horizontal placement guideline

Use Roxanne's to glue down the stem first. Place a berry at the end of the stem. Then place the 1/2" bias vine, checking to be sure the top of the stem is tucked under the vine. Make the inner curve fit smoothly and let the outer curve stretch to fit. Place a flower over one end of the 1/2" vine.

Move the placement template to an adjoining quarter of the background fabric and place another bias vine, stem, berry and flower. Move clockwise or counterclockwise around the block until you have worked on each quarter of the block.

Refer to the pattern to place the other berries. The outer leaves should be centered on the diagonal guidelines. Baste with Roxanne's glue as usual.

LESSONS FOR ADAPTING OTHER DESIGNS

Often you can make small changes to a pattern without detracting from the balance and beauty of the design. For example, if a design has 5/8" circles, you might change them to 1/2"" or 3/4" because those are standard sizes of the office dots that can be used as circle templates.

If you are working on a design with sharp inside angles, consider changing the angles to narrow inside curves. The slightly wider area of the curve will give you a little more seam allowance to turn under, strengthening the stability of the entire block.

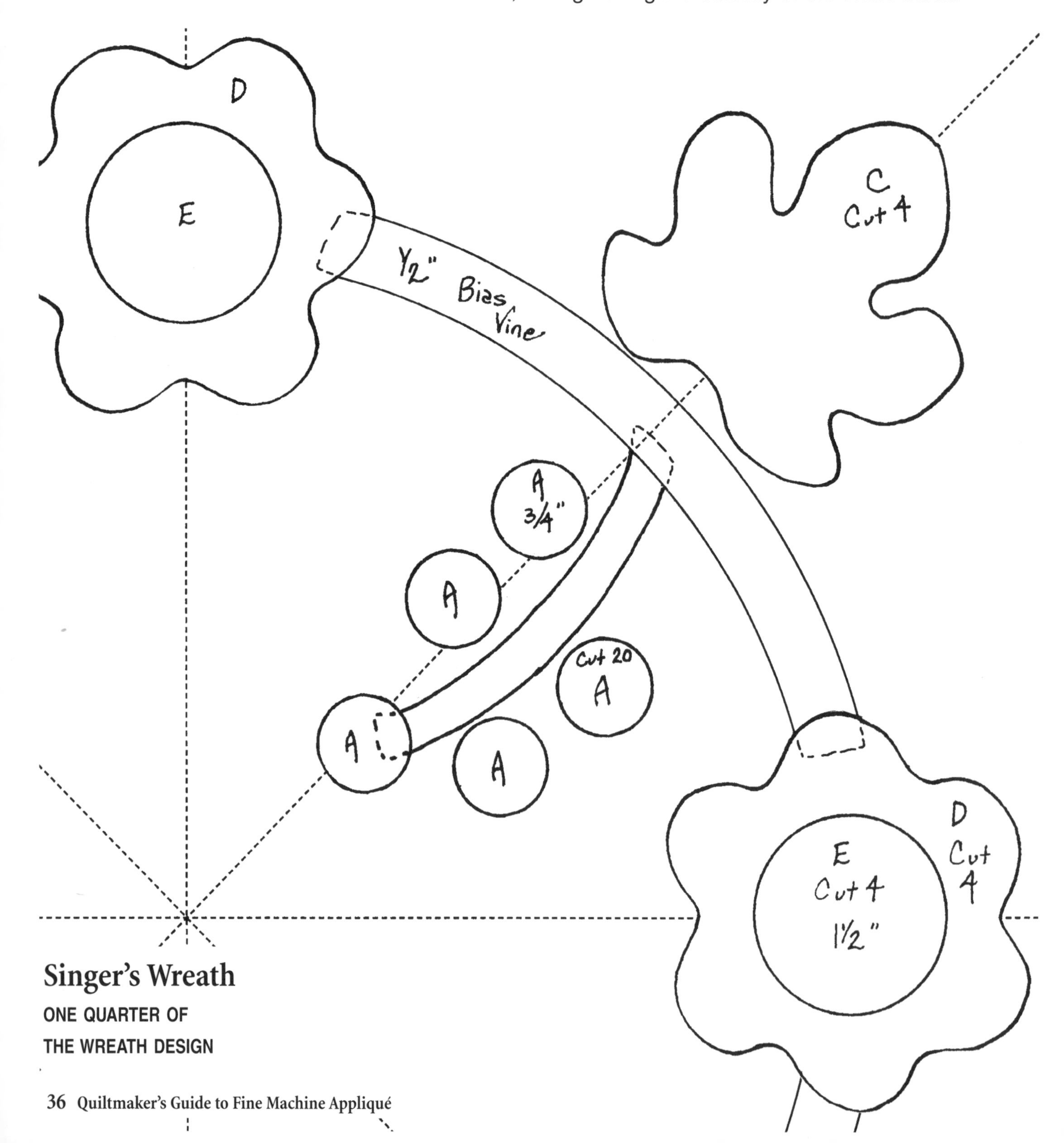

Singer's Wreath

ONE QUARTER OF THE WREATH DESIGN

Lesson 5 — Split Leaves

***Little Betty's Garden* block.**
Little Betty was a toy machine manufactured about 1890.

FABRIC REQUIREMENTS FOR THE *LITTLE BETTY'S GARDEN* BLOCK

- **Background fabric:** 16-1/2" square, cut oversized to be trimmed to 15-1/2" after appliqué is complete
- **Flower pot:** 6" x 8-1/2" rectangle. If you are using striped or other directional fabric, you may need extra.
- **Circles on flower pot:** 1-1/2" x 3-1/2" rectangle
- **Flower H:** 4-1/2" square
- **Flower G:** 3-1/2" square
- **Round center of flower H:** 2" square
- **Flower B:** 5" x 9" rectangle
- **Round center of flower B:** 2" x 4" rectangle
- **Small leaves:** 3" x 4" rectangle
- **Bud C:** 2-1/2" square
- **Caly x D:** 4-1/2" square
- **Top of split leaf:** 8" x 15" rectangle
- **Bottom of split leaf:** 6" x 7" rectangle
- **Stems:** 3-1/2" square. Cut three 3/4" bias strips to make 3/8" stems

MAKING THE SPLIT LEAF

- Turn under and glue the entire seam allowance of the top half of each leaf.
- Also glue under the lower edge of each bottom half, leaving the top edge open so it can be tucked under the top half of the leaf.
- Use Roxanne's to glue the bottom half of each leaf to the top half. Now you are ready to place the leaf on the block.

PREPARING AND SEWING THE BLOCK

By now you've learned how to prepare freezer-paper templates. cut, clip and turn under the edges of the appliqué pieces, position them on the background fabric, and sew them in place. Refer to the earlier lessons if you have questions.

LESSONS FOR ADAPTING OTHER DESIGNS

In every split image, the raw edge of one half tucks under the finished edge of the other half. In this case, we chose to tuck the bottom half of the leaf under the top half. Why? Because it is easier to glue under the seam allowance on the top half of the leaf. There is a very narrow, sharp point near the leaf's stem on the bottom half. By tucking that part of the leaf under the top half, you avoid turning under the seam allowance on both sides of the sharp point.

Split images add interest to appliqué designs. Feel free to split a leaf or flower that may not have been drawn that way in the original design. When you make the split image, examine both halves carefully to decide which edge should tuck under the other.

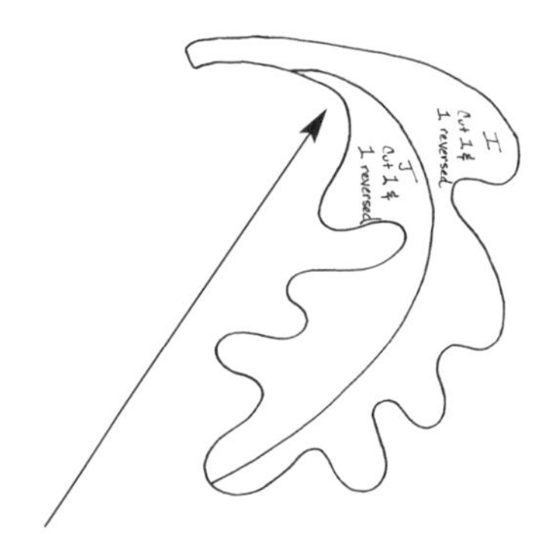

Avoid having to turn under both edges of this extremely sharp point by tucking the bottom half of the leaf under the top half.

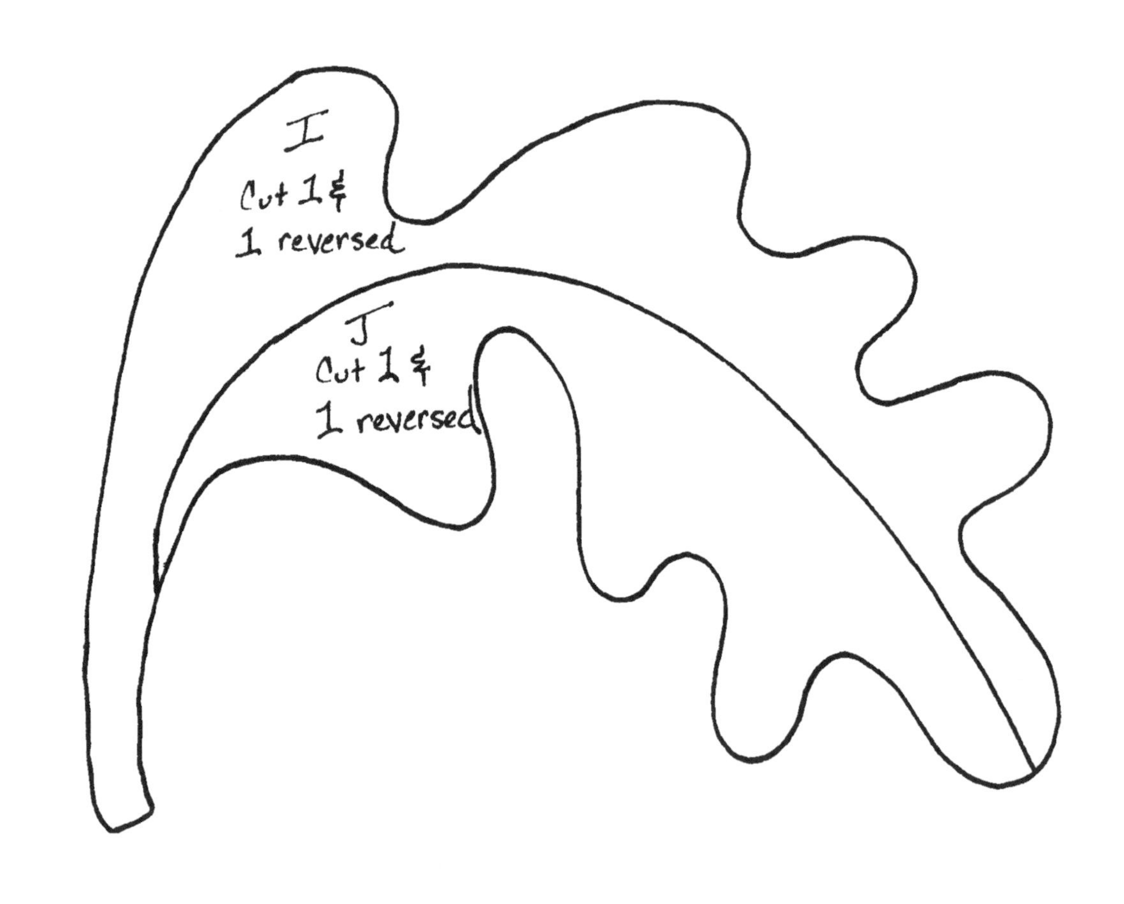

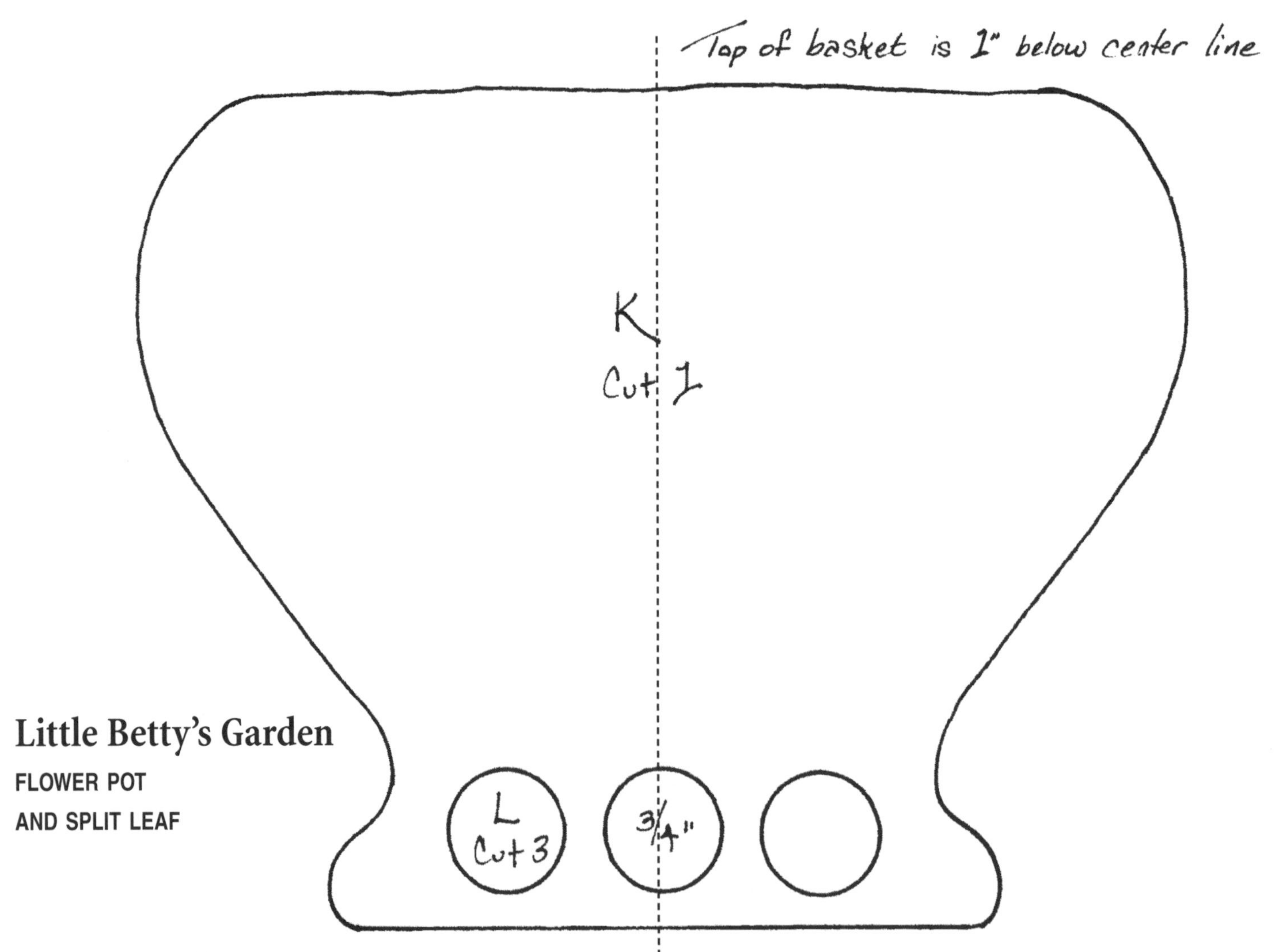

Little Betty's Garden

FLOWER POT
AND SPLIT LEAF

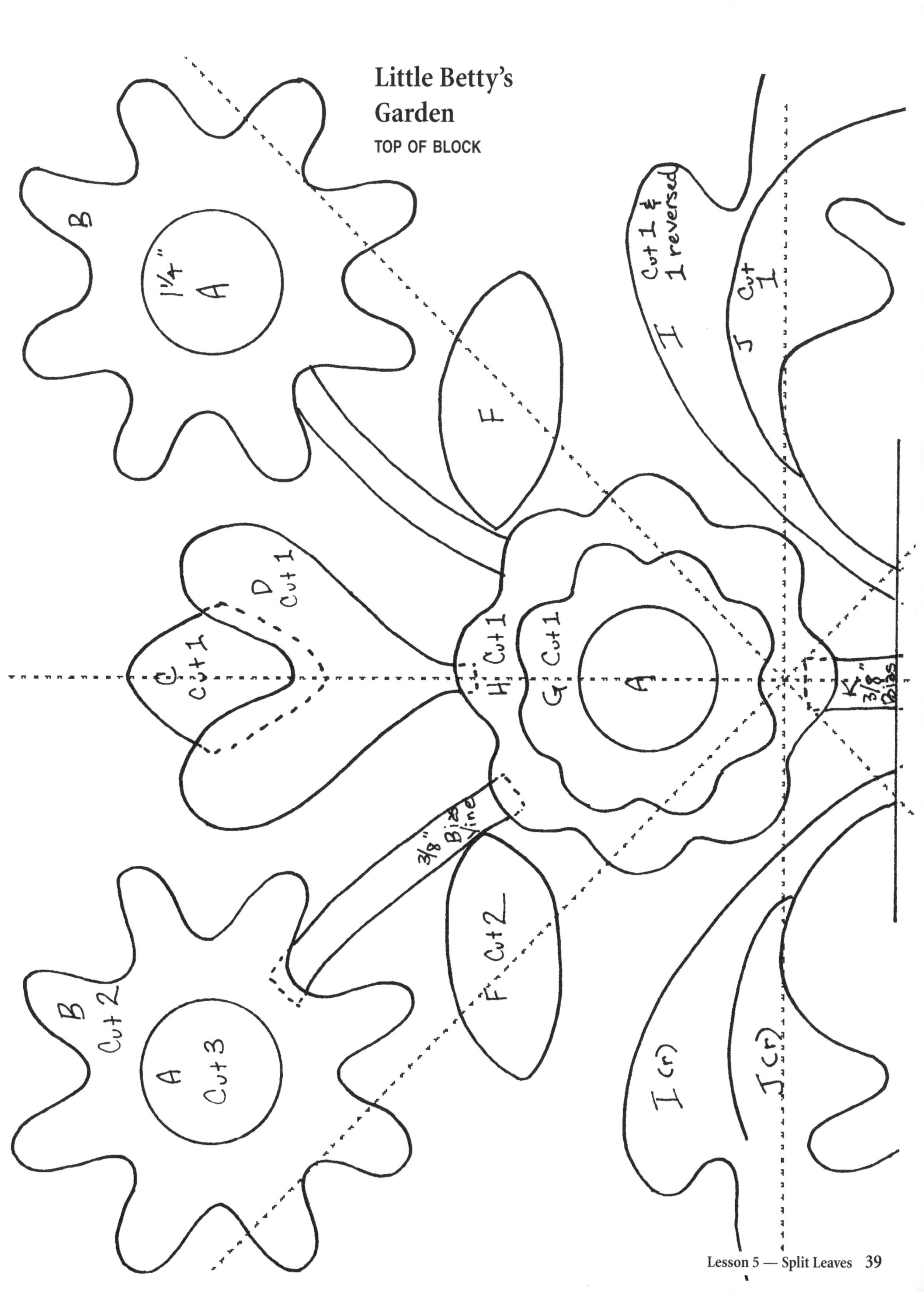
Little Betty's Garden
TOP OF BLOCK
B
A
F
D Cut 1
C Cut 1
H Cut 1
G Cut 1
A
F Cut 2
B Cut 2
A Cut 3
Cut 1 & 1 reversed
I
Cut 1
J
I (r)
J (r)

***Featherweight Wreath* block.**
Singer's *Featherweight* model was introduced at the Chicago World's Fair in the 1930s.

Lesson 6 — Reverse Appliqué

FABRIC REQUIREMENTS FOR THE *FEATHERWEIGHT WREATH* BLOCK

- **Background fabric:** 16-1/2" square, cut oversized to be trimmed to 15-1/2" after appliqué is complete
- **Leaf:** 16" square
- **Reversed center of leaf:** 7" x 6" rectangle
- **Reversed star:** 4-1/2" square
- **Small star for fake reverse appliqué:** 3-1/2" square

MAKING THE REVERSE APPLIQUÉ

- Achieving the reverse appliqué starts with preparation of the freezer paper. Cut out the inner reversed section of each leaf and the star.

- Iron the freezer paper onto the back of the fabric and cut the pieces out with a scant 1/4" seam allowance. Also cut the inner reverse sections with a 1/4" seam allowance.
- Glue under the outside and inside seam allowances on the leaves and the star.

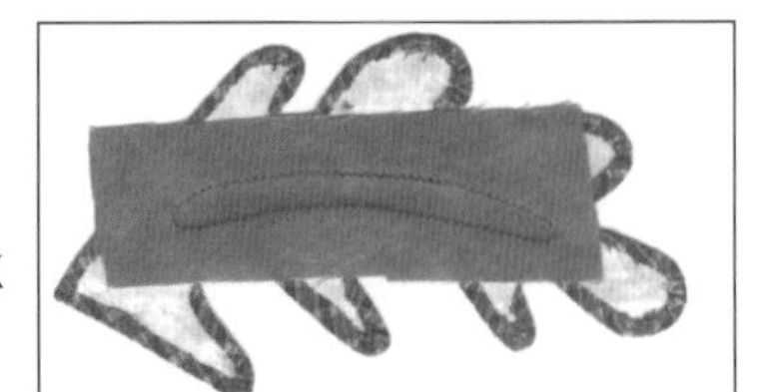

- To add another fabric to the inner reverse of the leaves, cut a 1-1/2" x 5" rectangle for each leaf. Lay the rectangle, right side up, on your work surface. Put some dots of Roxanne's glue on the inner seam allowance of the leaf, then place the leaf on top of the rectangle, checking to be sure that you have centered the inner reversed space on the rectangle. Machine appliqué the inner reverse, then trim away the excess fabric.

- To make the fake reverse-appliqué star shown in *New Century Sampler,* prepare an extra star using the inner reverse shape as a pattern. Glue under the outside edges of both stars, then glue the small star on top of the large star. As with all layered designs, remember to appliqué the top star to the bottom star before you place them on the background fabric.

PREPARING AND SEWING THE BLOCK

By now you've learned how to prepare freezer-paper templates. cut, clip and turn under the edges of the appliqué pieces, position them on the background fabric, and sew them in place. Use a quarter-block placement template, like those in Lessons 2 and 4, for this block. Refer to the earlier lessons if you have questions.

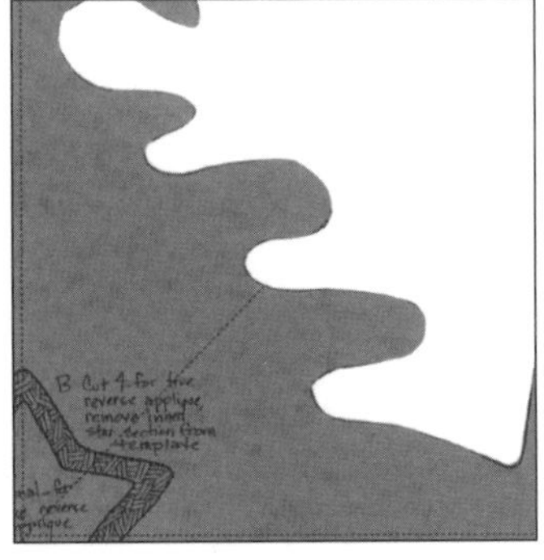

Make a placement template for this block.

LESSONS FOR ADAPTING OTHER DESIGNS

Now that you've learned how easy reverse appliqué can be, you may want to try more reverse appliqué designs. Many antique quilt designs include very small reversed areas that do not have much space for turning under a seam allowance. Feel free to use the "fake reverse appliqué" technique in those cases.

And remember that you can change sharp inside angles to narrow inner curves to allow more room for turning under an adequate seam allowance.

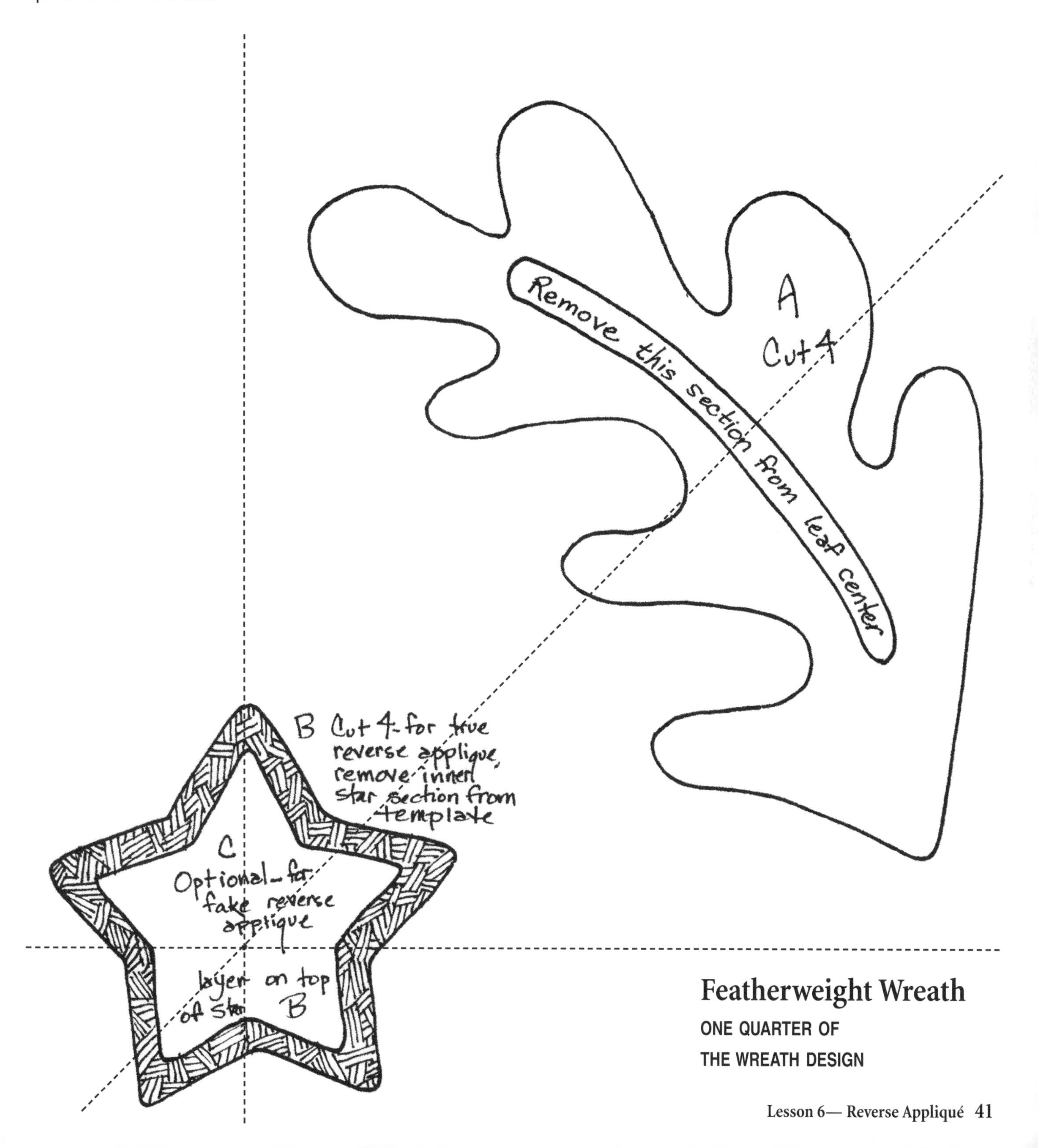

Featherweight Wreath

ONE QUARTER OF THE WREATH DESIGN

***Jenny Lind's Garden* block.** *Jenny Lind* was the earliest Singer machine model, manufactured in 1851. These first Singers cost about $125.

Lesson 7 — Open-Work Appliqué

FABRIC REQUIREMENTS FOR THE *JENNY LIND'S GARDEN* BLOCK

- **Background fabric:** 16-1/2" square, cut oversized to be trimmed to 15-1/2" after appliqué is complete
- **Flower pot:** 6" x 11" rectangle for the sides, upright pieces, and bottom. Plus 6" x 7" rectangle for the horizontal slats.
- **Large flower**: 6" x 4" rectangle
- **Circles on large flower:** 1" x 5" rectangle
- **Calyx of large flower:** 4-1/2" square
- **Flower F:** 3" x 6" rectangle
- **Flower E**: 3" x 5" rectangle
- **Flower H:** 3-1/2" x 7" rectangle
- **Flower G:** 2-1/2" x 5" rectangle
- **Stems and leaves:** 7" x 12" rectangle

MAKING THE OPEN-WORK BASKET

- First, make the freezer paper templates. Trace and cut out the side pieces of the basket. For the other basket parts, cut 1/2" strips of freezer paper and trim them to length for the basket cross-pieces. Label each one. Trim three more lengths for the basket uprights and refer to the pattern to round one end of each.
- Place the pattern templates on the diagonal grain of the fabric, iron and cut out as usual.
- Glue under the entire seam allowance of the side pieces, but leave the ends of the cross pieces and the bottoms of the uprights free to tuck under another piece.
- Photocopy or trace the basket pattern on a separate piece of paper. Pin the cross pieces in place on the pattern sheet
- Put a few dots of Roxanne's on the left seam allowance of every cross piece and set the left side piece in place. For now, also pin it to the paper pattern.
- Take the straight pins out of the cross pieces. Weave the first upright piece into the cross pieces, using the tip of the Roxanne's to put some glue under each intersection.

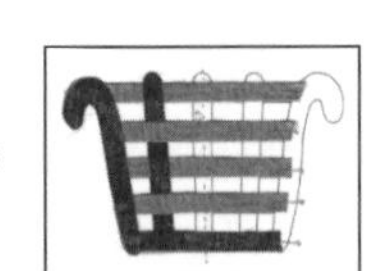

- Weave the second and third upright pieces into the basket in the same manner.

- Put a few dots of Roxanne's on the right seam allowance of every cross piece and set the side piece in place. Let the glue dry for 5 minutes. Pick up the assembled basket and place it on the background fabric.

PREPARING AND SEWING THE BLOCK

You have several choices about how to make the stems.

1. You can cut freezer paper templates for the stems, iron them onto the back of the fabric, and glue as usual. This option makes block layout easy, because the curve of the long stems is built into the pattern pieces. However, the stems are fairly narrow. To reduce the chance of raveling, cut the stems on the bias of the fabric.
2. Cut freezer paper templates, but iron them on top of the fabric and use them as a guide to folding under the seam allowance. The advantage of this choice is that you will not need to cut open the background fabric behind the stems to remove the freezer paper. The disadvantage is that it takes extra time and skill to fold the seam allowance away from the paper, and the soft edge of the resulting shape is more difficult to machine stitch accurately.
3. You can make bias tape stems — 3/8" bias for the central stem and 1/4" bias for the other stems. Bias tape stems are easy to make. See directions on page 16. However, pattern placement will be slightly more difficult because you will have to curve the bias stems to match the pattern drawing.

   This is the option we chose. If you use bias tape stems, make a modified placement template showing the curve of the long stem in relationship to the basket top.

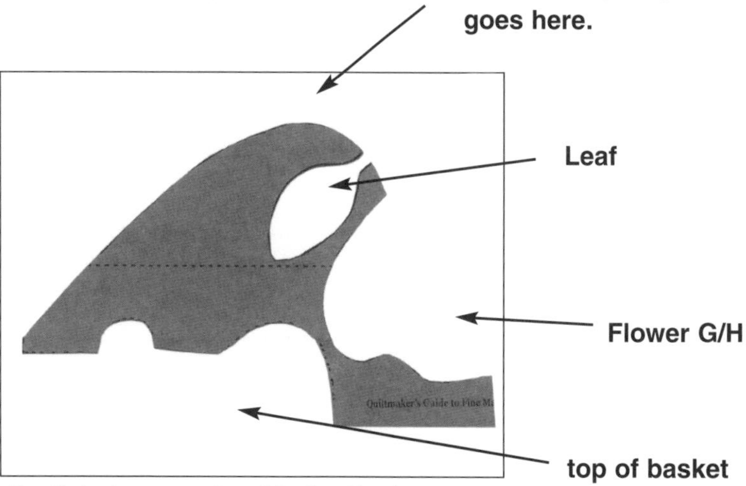

Partial placement guide for the long curved stem

By now you've learned the rest of what you need to know to make this block. Refer to the earlier lessons if you have questions.

LESSONS FOR ADAPTING OTHER DESIGNS

Choosing when to use bias tape stems and when to cut them from freezer paper is mostly a matter of personal choice. When cutting the background fabric out to remove the freezer paper, it's best to avoid having to cut a slit that is 1/4" or narrower because the slit would leave a seam allowance of only 1/8" or less.

Using a freezer paper template can ensure the accuracy of a design shape, however, and cutting the shape on the bias of the fabric helps reduce the raveling you might expect from a narrow seam allowance. Washing the glue out of the block before you cut the background behind a narrow appliqué shape also helps cut down on raveling.

Choose the option that you think will give you the best results.

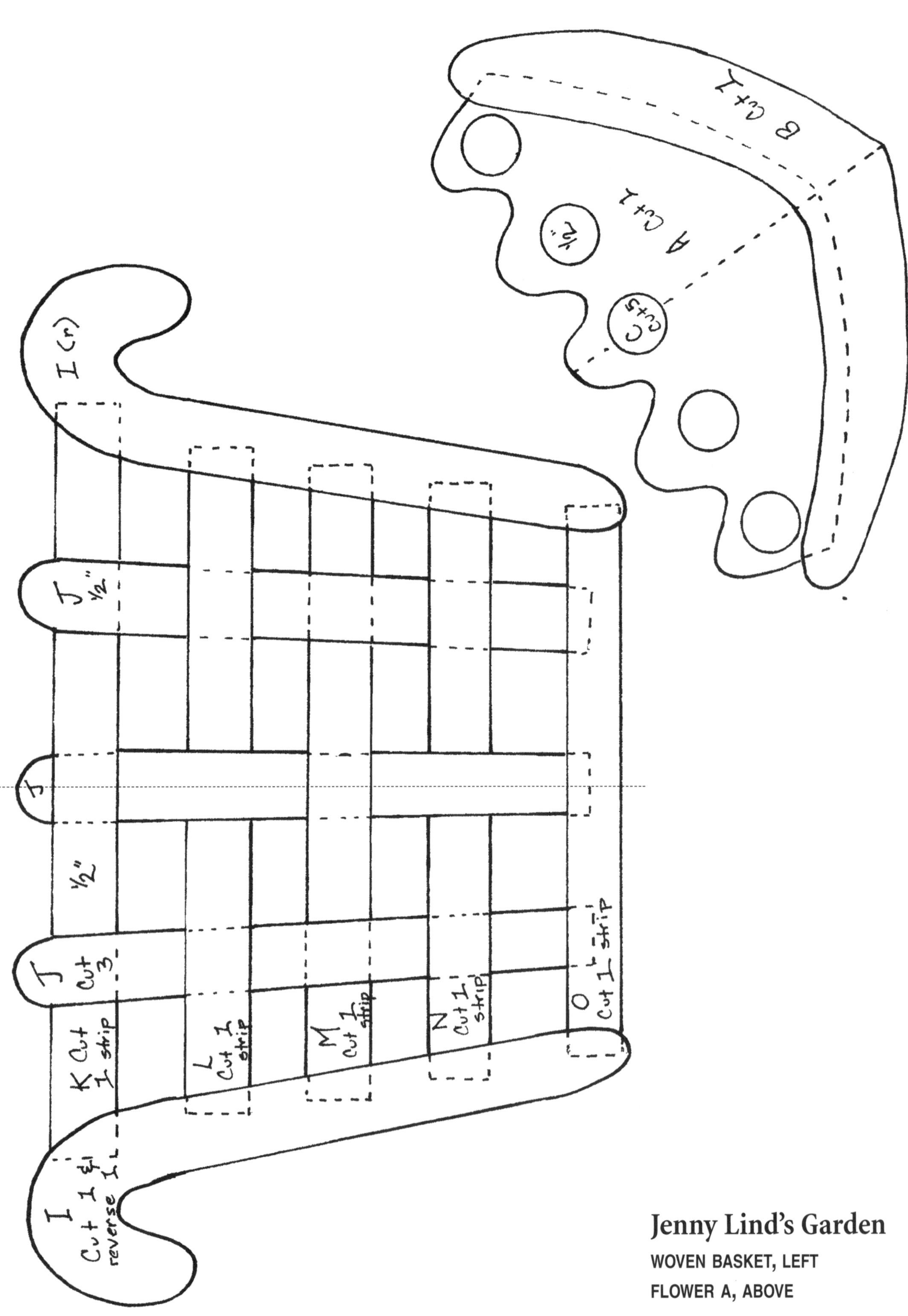

Jenny Lind's Garden

WOVEN BASKET, LEFT

FLOWER A, ABOVE

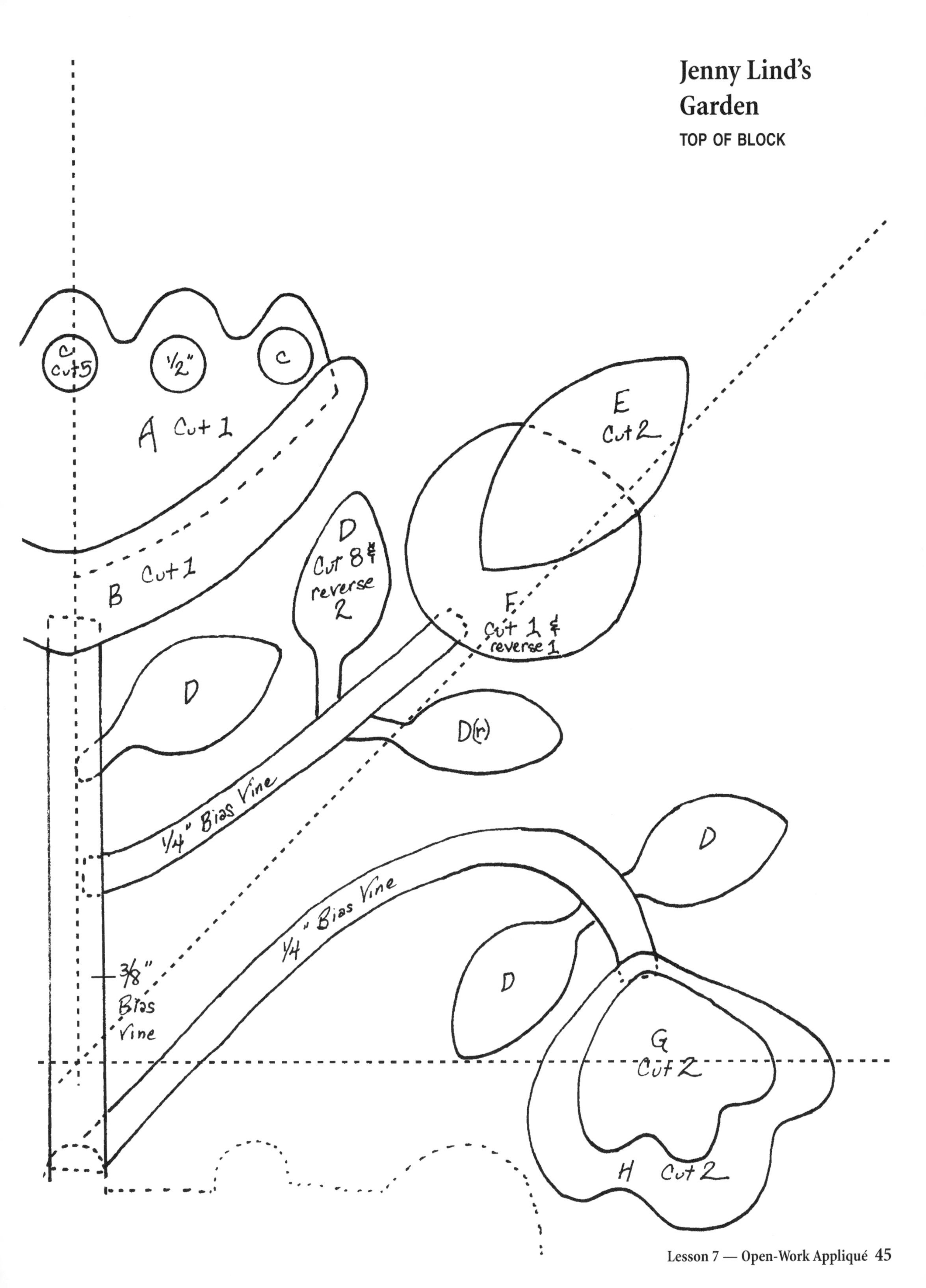

Jenny Lind's Garden

TOP OF BLOCK

***Betsy Ross's Wreath* block.** *Betsy Ross* **was a toy machine, named for the seamstress reputed to have stitched America's first flag.**

Lesson 8 — Combined Techniques

FABRIC REQUIREMENTS FOR THE *BETSY ROSS'S WREATH* BLOCK

- **Background fabric:** 16-1/2" square, cut oversized to be trimmed to 15-1/2" after appliqué is complete
- **Flag stripes:** 4-1/2" x 9" rectangle
- **Flag star field:** 3" x 6" rectangle
- **Flag poles:** 4-1/2" square
- **Flag stripes:** 4-1/2" x 9" rectangle
- **Vine:** 6" square
- **Berries:** 5" x 8" rectangle
- **Star background:** 4" x 6"
- **Star points:** 6 scraps, each at least 2" square

MAKING THE PIECED STAR IN A CIRCLE

This little star in a circle is a tough piecing job. Freezer paper piecing — using freezer paper templates as seam guides — is the perfect way to put it together accurately.

If you haven't tried this technique before, we warn you that this is a small piece for a beginner. But we think you'll recognize the advantages of freezer paper piecing, a technique used by many quilt artists to put together complex images.

The marriage of freezer paper piecing and machine appliqué is a happy union. When the piecing is finished, the freezer paper edges can be glued under to make it ready to be appliquéd.

If this is your first experience with freezer paper piecing or you don't like working with small shapes, you could combine pieces D< E, and F to eliminate some of the seams.

- Trace or photocopy the star-in-a-circle pattern. Stack the drawing on top of the shiny side of a piece of freezer paper. Use the iron to tack the two sheets of paper together.
- Use small scissors to carefully cut out the circle. Then use a rotary cutter and ruler to cut apart the pattern pieces. Mark the pattern letter on each template.
- The pieces with a curved edge — A, C, K, I, and G — form the background of the star and can be cut from the same piece of fabric. The other pieces form the star and can be cut from scraps. Iron the templates on the back of the fabric and use a rotary cutter and ruler to cut them out with exact 1/4" seam allowances.
- Arrange the pieces face down, in order, on your sewing machine table. Because you will be looking at the back of the block, the arrangement of the letter codes will be reversed from the pattern. Pieces A, D and G will be on the right and Pieces C, F and K will be on the left. (fig. 1)

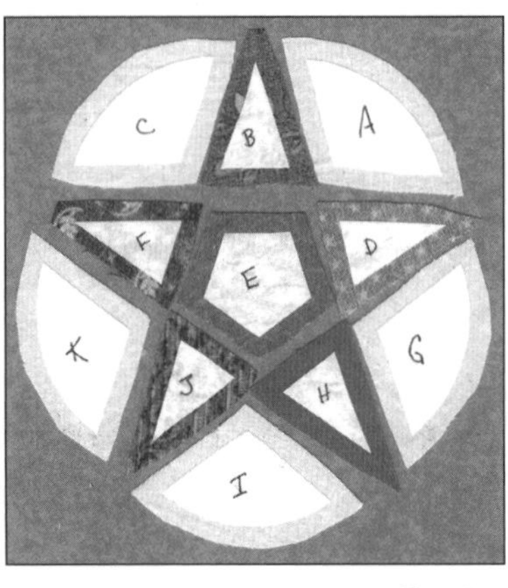

fig. 1

- Use the edges of the freezer paper templates as pinning and sewing guides. Pin and sew the pieces together in sets: ABC, DEF, GH, IJK. (fig. 2)
- Sew set GH to the bottom of set DEF. (fig. 3)
- Sew set ABC to the top of set DEFGH.
- Sew set IJK to the bottom of the partially assembled star.
- Trim the seam allowances to a little more than 1/8", then use a glue stick to turn under the edge. Now it's ready to appliqué. (fig. 4)

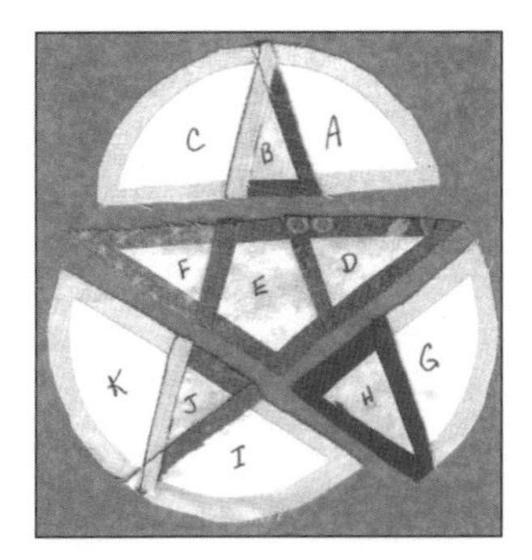

fig. 2

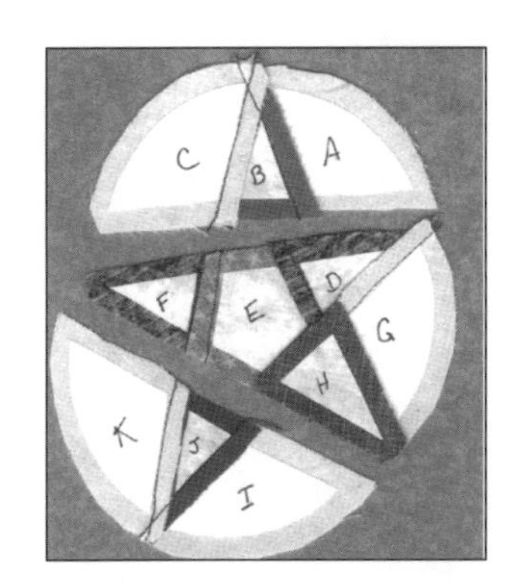

fig. 3

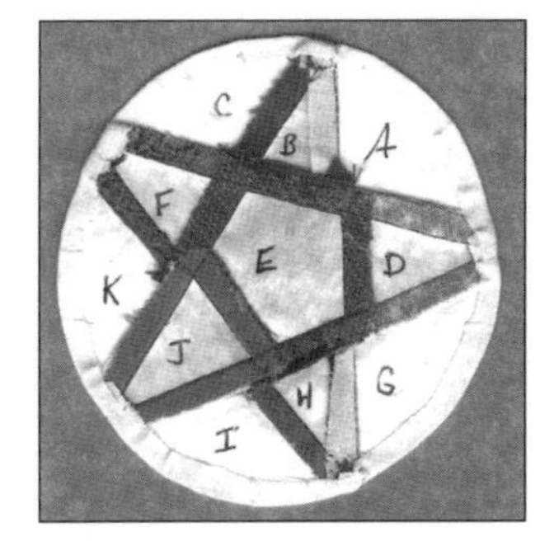

fig. 4

PREPARING AND SEWING THE BLOCK

By now you've learned how to prepare freezer-paper templates. cut, clip and turn under the edges of the appliqué pieces, position them on the background fabric, and sew them in place. Just a few notes:

The curve of the bias vine in this block is so sharp that it would be difficult to place a 1/4" bias tape vine smoothly. Make freezer paper templates for the vines instead.

Use Roxanne's to assemble the flags before you place them on the background fabric.

Refer to the block's horizontal, vertical and diagonal placement guidelines to help you place the pieces on the background. Be sure to tuck the ends of the vines and the flag poles under the center star.

Refer to the earlier lessons if you have questions.

LESSONS FOR ADAPTING OTHER DESIGNS

Karla combined freezer paper techniques on her first quilt for the Sunflower Pattern Co-operative, when she pieced the dog house for the sampler quilt *War and Pieces* and appliquéd its edges to the *Loyal Dog* block.

Using freezer paper as a piecing template eliminates the need to trace template lines on the fabric. In addition, the freezer paper prevents seam distortion by holding bias edges in place during sewing. Combining freezer paper techniques makes it possible for you to make almost any quilt you can design.

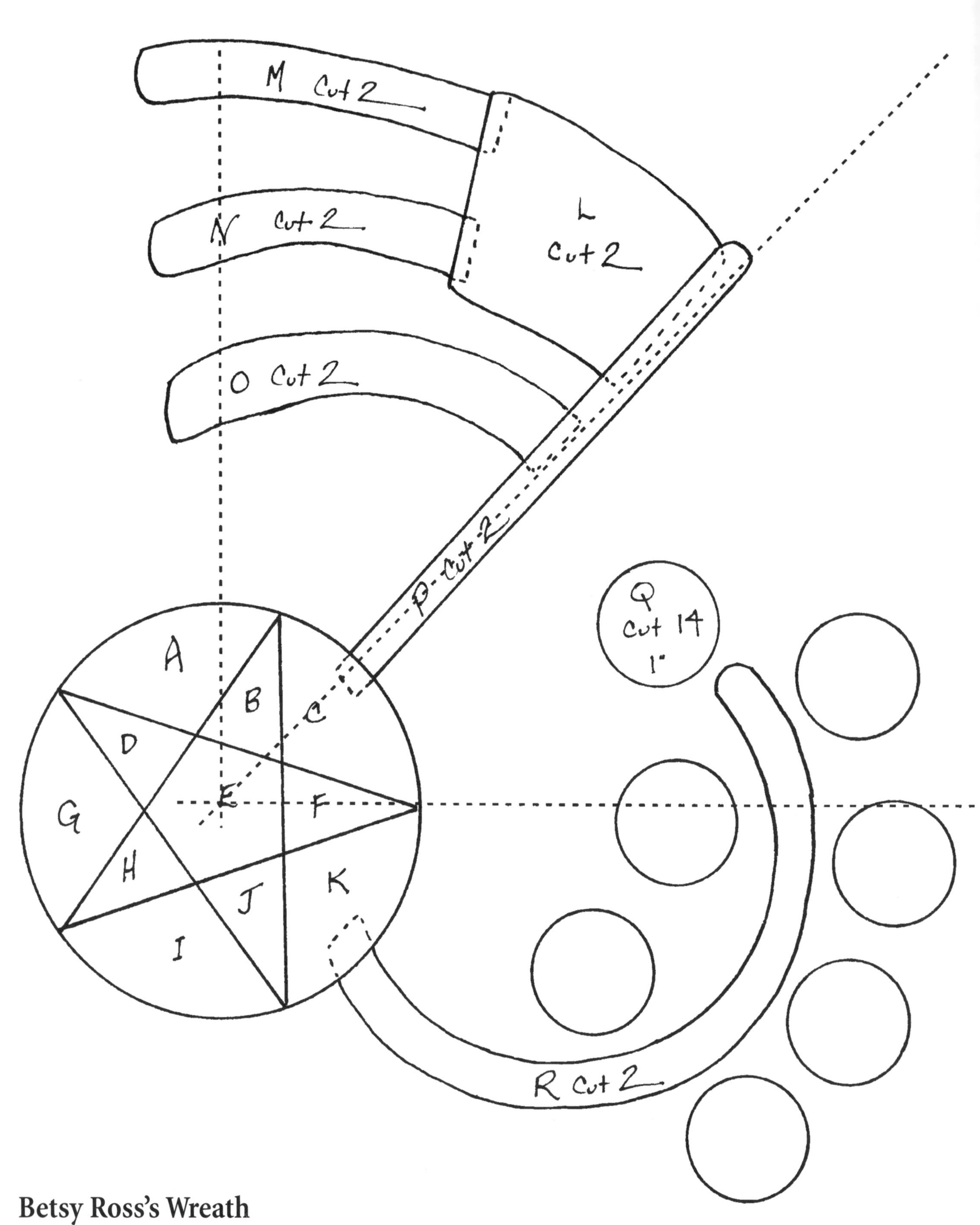

Betsy Ross's Wreath

ONE QUARTER OF
THE WREATH DESIGN

Lesson 9 — Strip-Pieced Leaves

FABRIC REQUIREMENTS FOR THE *NEW QUEEN'S GARDEN* BLOCK

- **Background fabric:** 16-1/2" square, cut oversized to be trimmed to 15-1/2" after appliqué is complete
- **Flower basket and handle:** 9" x 12" rectangle. If you are using striped or other directional fabric, you may need extra.
- **Circles on basket:** 2-1/2" x 7-1/2" rectangle
- **Stems:** 4" x 6" rectangle
- **Flower M:** 3-1/2" x 7" rectangle
- **Flower center N:** 2" x 4" rectangle
- **Round center of flower M:** 1-1/2" x 3" rectangle
- **Leaves D and G:** 4-1/2" square
- **Pieced leaves and bud:** 6" square of pieced or striped fabric

***New Queen's Garden* block.** *New Queen* was a brand of Sears, Roebuck and Company. In 1902 a *New Queen* machine in a cabinet sold for $10.45.

MAKING THE STRIP-PIECED LEAVES

- Cut six to eight 6" strips, ranging in width from 3/4" to 1-1/4". It's better if the strips are not even. Cut straight edges, but wider at one end than the other.
- Seam the strips together into a square approximately 6" and iron the seams to one side. You can iron the seams open to make flatter leaves. But the open seam lines would be weak points in the finished quilt top.

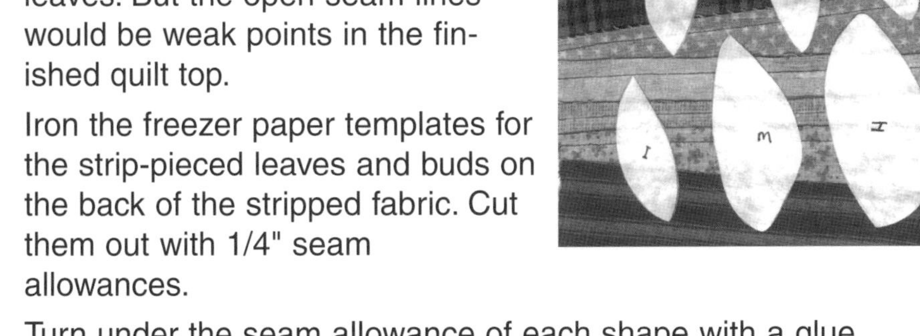

- Iron the freezer paper templates for the strip-pieced leaves and buds on the back of the stripped fabric. Cut them out with 1/4" seam allowances.
- Turn under the seam allowance of each shape with a glue stick. You will need to put extra glue at the seam lines to help hold down the multiple layers of the seam allowance. Be sure that the edges of each shape are firmly glued. The presser foot will put extra pressure on the seam lines while you stitch them to the background, so the edges need to be securely in place before you sew.

PREPARING AND SEWING THE BLOCK

By now you've learned how to prepare freezer-paper templates. cut, clip and turn under the edges of the appliqué pieces, position them on the background fabric, and sew them in place. A note: Cut the basket handle with a freezer paper template instead of using bias tape. It would be difficult to place bias tape smoothly around the handle's deep curve. Refer to the earlier lessons if you have questions.

LESSONS FOR ADAPTING OTHER DESIGNS

Piecing a scrappy square is much less tedious than sewing together small scraps for each appliqué shape. If you don't like working with the fat seams on the strip-pieced leaves but you like the look, try using striped fabric instead.

Since the pieced fabric is bulky, try to use it with simple shapes that have rounded or blunt points.

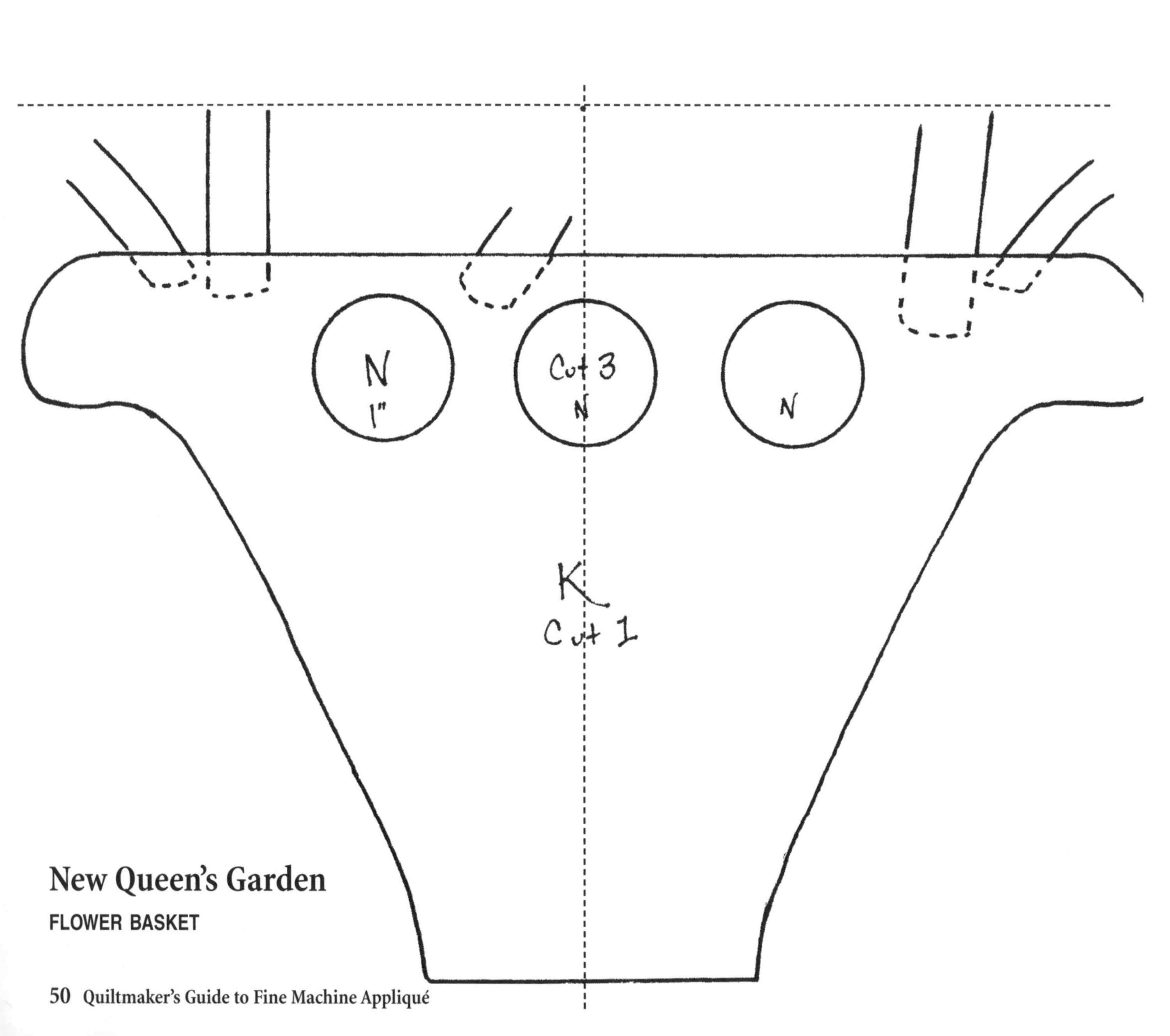

New Queen's Garden

FLOWER BASKET

New Queen's Garden

TOP OF BLOCK

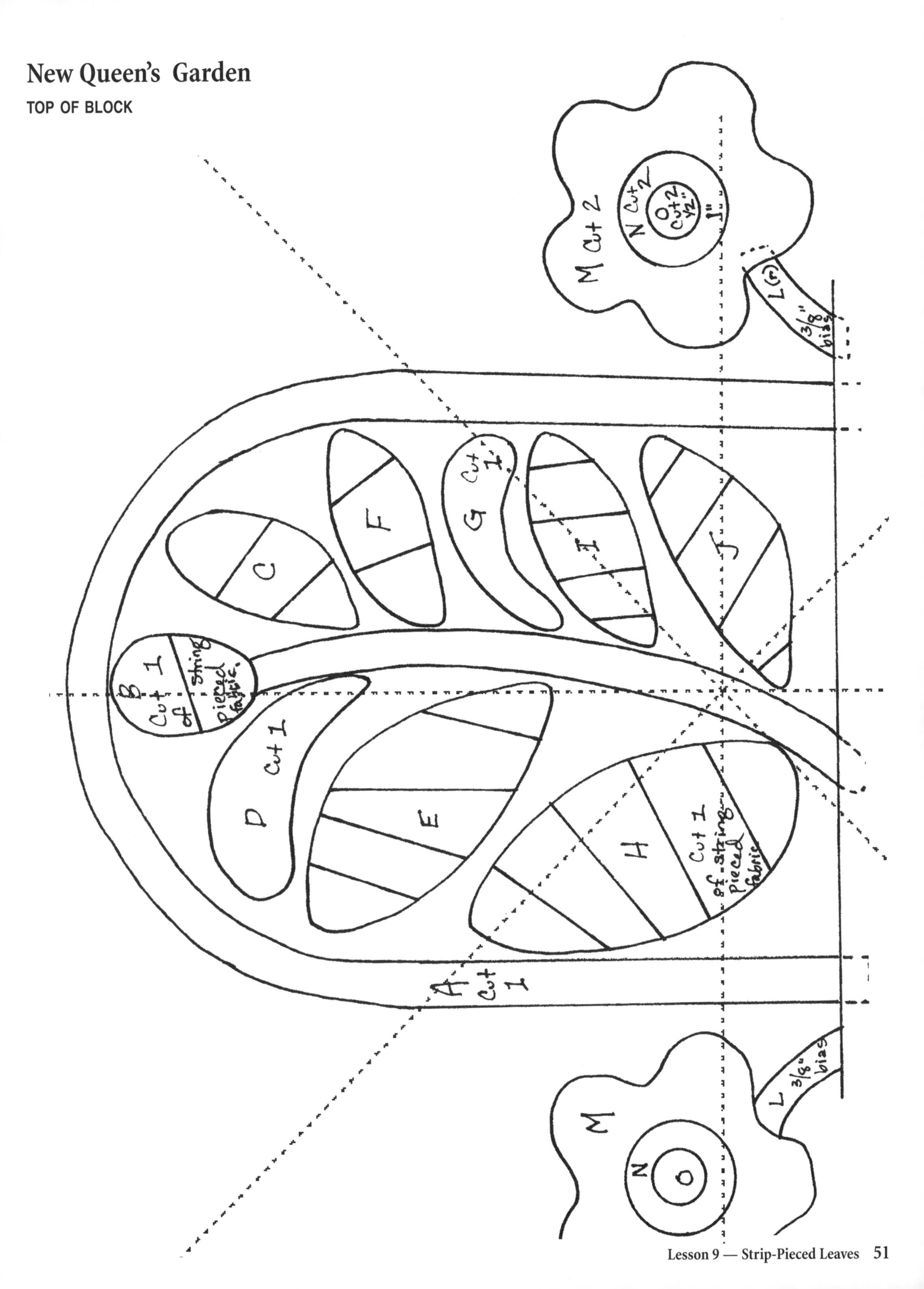

Lesson 10 — Dogtooth Border

NEW CENTURY SAMPLER

- **50" square sampler**
- **15" square blocks**
- **2-1/2" finished dogtooth border**

FABRIC REQUIREMENTS FOR THE *DOGTOOTH BORDER*

- **Background fabric:** two 3" x 50-1/2" strips and two 3" x 45-1/2" strips, as directed in cutting instructions on page 19
- **Red for dogtooth border:** 1/2 yard

PUTTING THE QUILT TOGETHER

Wash the blocks and take out the freezer paper as described on page 17. Trim each to 15-1/2" and sew them together as shown in the photo at left. The quilt body should be 45-1/2" square.

Adding the dogtooth border may seem a little confusing to you if you have never worked with an appliquéd border. From the background fabric, you will make two short borders to add to the sides of the quilt and two long borders to add to the top and bottom. The width of the top and bottom borders adds to the length of the side borders, making each side of the finished top the same size. That means that each side must have the same number of dogteeth, even though you won't be able to appliqué all of the side-border sawteeth until the borders are sewn onto the quilt.

MAKING THE DOGTOOTH BORDER

- Cut the red fabric into five strips 3" x the width of the fabric. Piece the strips together to make four 50-1/2" strips.
- Cut four strips of freezer paper 2-1/2" wide x 50" long.
- Trace the dogtooth pattern on page 53 onto one end of each freezer paper strip. Line up the grey base of the pattern with the horizontal and vertical edges of the freezer paper strips.
- Accordion-fold the freezer paper strips in 10" segments. Make the folds precisely at the edge of the dogtooth pattern. There should be five layers. Staple within each grey dogtooth to hold the strips together.

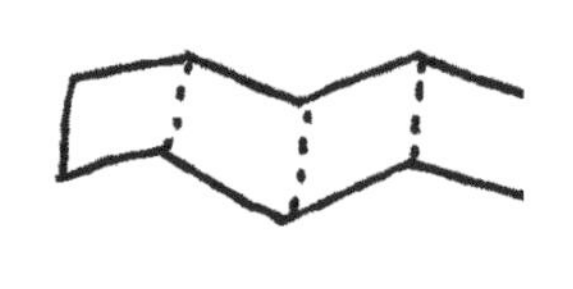

- Cut along the pattern lines. Unfold the freezer paper. You will have four 2-1/2" x 50" dogtooth templates, each with 25 dogteeth. On each strip, cut off and discard the last two dogteeth so each strip has 23 dogteeth.
- Iron the dogtooth templates onto the back of the fabric strips, aligning the straight edges of the paper and the fabric. The fabric strips are 1/2" longer than the paper, so leave 1/4" seam allowance at each end of the strips.
- Cut out the dogtooth fabric, leaving a 1/4" seam allowance around each point. Make one clip into each inner angle.
- Glue under the seam allowance. Fold and glue the tip of each dogtooth first, then glue under one side of each dogtooth. Glue under the other side of each dogtooth, using the stiletto to nudge any extending seam allowance back under the point.

- Mark the horizontal center of each background strip and the horizontal center of each dogtooth strip.
- Place a glued dogtooth strip on each 51" background strip, matching the horizontal center marks and aligning the straight edge of the dogteeth with the long straight edge of the background strip. Use Roxanne's Glu-Baste-It to adhere the dogtooth strips to the background.
- Place a glued dogtooth strip on each 46" background strip, matching the horizontal center marks and aligning the straight edge of the dogteeth with the long straight edge of the background strip. You'll notice that the dogtooth strips are longer than the background strips. Don't worry; they are supposed to be. Use Roxanne's Glu-Baste-It to adhere the 21 middle dogteeth to the background, leaving the outer dogteeth free at each end of the strips.
- Appliqué the dogteeth in place. On the two short borders, stitch only the 21 middle dogteeth to the background for now.
- Pin a short border to each side of the quilt, matching the border center with the center of a quilt side. The dogteeth should point toward the center of the quilt. Sew the short borders to the sides of the quilt. Pin the excess dogteeth back to expose the short ends of the background strips.
- Pin the long borders to the top and bottom of the quilt, matching the centers and making the dogteeth point toward the quilt center. Sew the borders to the quilt.
- Now that the entire border is sewn onto the quilt, you can finish appliquéing the dogteeth. Use the Roxanne's to finish gluing the dogteeth to the border corners and appliqué them in place.
- To finish the corners, cut four 2-1/2" squares of freezer paper and iron them onto the back of the extra red dogtooth fabric. Cut them out with 1/4" seam allowance on two adjoining sides. Glue under the two seam allowances on each square.

  Place a square in each corner of the quilt. We've designed the squares to be oversized so that you can adjust the placement of each to make the corners look good. The corners may be slightly inconsistent, but that will not be very noticeable in the finished quilt. After you are pleased with the placement of the squares, glue-baste in place and appliqué. Trim the excess seam allowance to square up the corners.

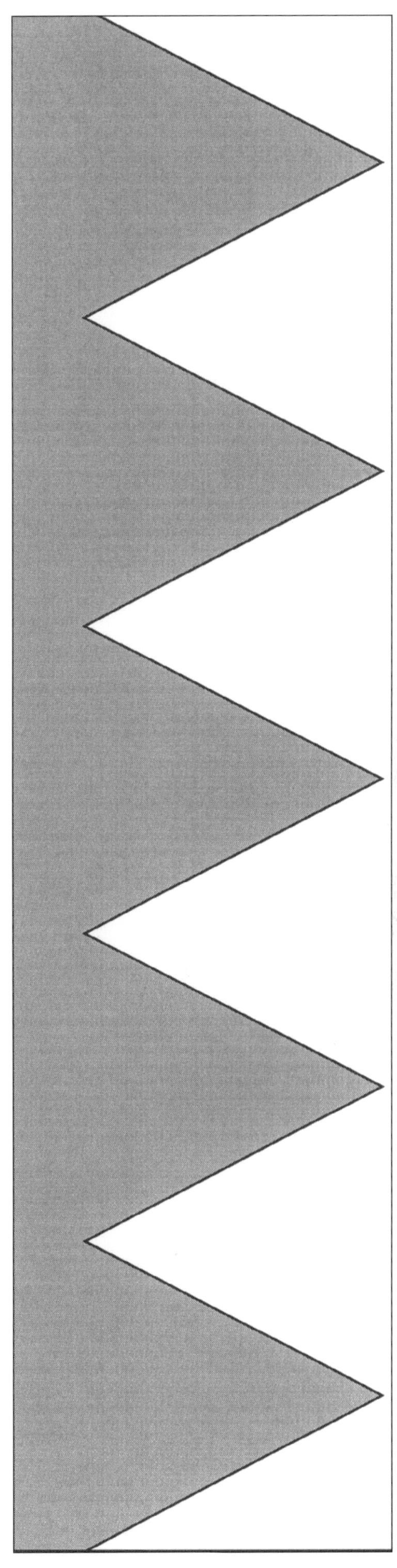

TAKING OUT THE BORDER FREEZER PAPER

Whenever possible, we recommend washing completed appliqué to thoroughly remove the glue and to take the paper out. But quilt borders are an exception.

It would be impractical to wash the quilt top after the border is attached because the seam allowances would fray. And it would not be practical to wash the borders before they are sewn onto the quilt because the appliqué that goes into the border corners has to remain unstitched until the borders are sewn onto the quilt.

Instead, use a spray bottle of water to get each border thoroughly wet. Remove the freezer paper, then put the quilt top — dry blocks and wet border — into the clothes dryer. Put a dry clean towel in with the quilt to help absorb some of the excess water. After the borders are dry, iron the quilt top. You can trim away the excess border behind the sawteeth if you wish.

LESSONS FOR ADAPTING OTHER DESIGNS

Many great quilt patterns have dogtooth designs. Some are evenly spaced like this one to fit the border. Others look hand-drawn, only loosely based on the measurements of the border. To design your own, refer to the cross-section of a dogtooth shown below to plan your design. The grey area represents the freezer paper template. The white area shows the additional seam allowance of the fabric strip.

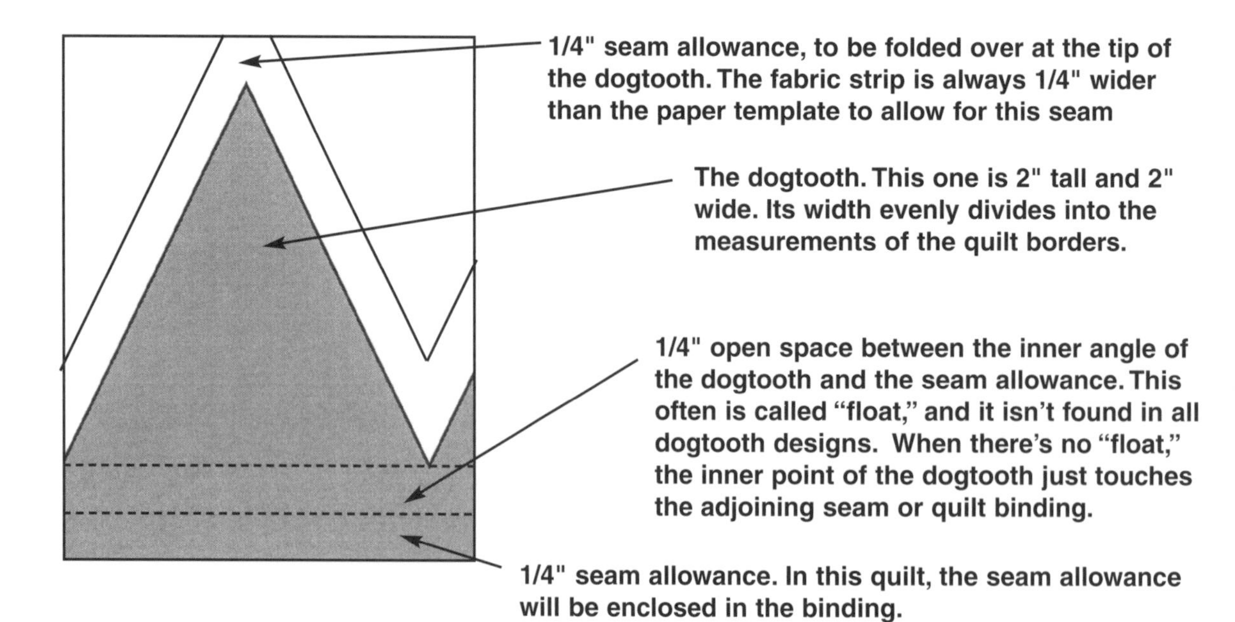

Lesson 11 — Appliqué Border

NEW CENTURY GARDEN

- **65" square sampler**
- **15" blocks**
- **10" finished floral border**

FABRIC REQUIREMENTS FOR THE APPLIQUÉ BORDER

- **Background fabric:** Two 10-1/2" x 45-1/2" strips and two 10-1/2" x 65-1/2" strips, as directed in cutting instructions on page 18.
- **Medium brown bias vine:** 1" bias strips from the same yardage as the block fabric, as directed in the cutting instructions on page 18. Buy 2/3 yard if you use different fabric.
- **Green bias vine:** Several 3/4" bias strips totaling 40"
- **Appliquéd flowers and leaves:** Use the yardage left over from the quilt blocks. Be sure to include the leftover block background fabric in the border appliqué pieces. We used the medium brown fabric for the border vine and some leaves and the dark brown block fabric for the side-border flower pots.

PUTTING THE QUILT TOGETHER

Wash the blocks and take out the freezer paper as described on page 15. Trim each to 15-1/2" and sew them together as shown in the photo at right. The quilt body should be 45-1/2" square.

Like the dogtooth border, this border's appliqué extends into the border corners. Our construction method will teach you how to appliqué as much as possible before the borders are sewn onto the quilt, leaving the corner appliqué to be finished after the quilt is fully constructed.

PREPARING THE APPLIQUÉ BORDER

Prepare the appliqué shapes as instructed in the earlier lessons. You will need

- From Lesson 2, four stars
- From Lesson 3, two flower pots and four each leaf C, leaf C(r), leaf D, and leaf D(r)
- From Lesson 5, two flower pots, one split leaf, one split leaf (r), 14 flower B/A, and one flower H/G/A
- From Lesson 7, four flower A/B/C and seven flower H/G
- From Lesson 8, two flags and 2 flags (r)
- From Lesson 9, eight leaf H and eight leaf H(r)

Appliqué the circles to the flower pots from Lesson 5 and the top layers to the base of the multi-layered flowers from all the blocks.

Use Roxanne's glue to baste together the flower pots and borders from Lesson 3, flower ABC from Lesson 7, the split leaves and the flags. Set the shapes aside while you prepare the rest of the border.

Make the bias vine. Use a 1/2" bias tape maker to fold under the edges of the 1" brown bias strips. Trim eight of the strips to 32" in length to be used for the main border vine. Use the leftover vine for flower stems. Use a 3/8" bias tape maker to fold under the edges of the 3/4" green strips. These also will be used as flower stems.

Machine baste the border to the quilt body. Baste the side borders on first, then the top and bottom borders. This will make it easier for you to place the appliqué shapes accurately.

BORDER APPLIQUÉ PLACEMENT

Follow this step-by-step process to learn how to arrange border elements without following an exact pattern.

- Put the quilt top on a design wall or lay it on a flat surface. Mark the center points of each border.
- Pin a flower pot in the center of each border. The top of the pot should face the center of the quilt, with the bottom 3/4" from the outer edge of the border.
- Pin a flower A/B from Lesson 5 in each border corner. Make the placement the same distance from the border edges in each corner.
- Referring to the photograph on the previous page, place the split leaves and the large, three-part flower from Lesson 5 in the pot on the bottom border. Put a 3/8" green stem between the flower pot and the large flower.
- Place one of the 1/2" brown bias vines on the bottom border. Tuck one end of the vine under the top of the flower pot, between the flower stem and a split leaf. Arrange the vine to gently curve up from the flower pot, then sweep downward to end under the flower you have pinned in the border corner. Pin the vine in place.
- Referring to the quilt photo, pin the other appliqué elements onto the same side of the bottom border to see if the vine placement has left enough room for the other elements. Make adjustments if necessary.
- Cut a piece of freezer paper at least 11" wide x 40" long. Align a long edge of the freezer paper with the seam line between the quilt border and the quilt body, covering the bottom flower pot and the side of the border that you have just designed. The shiny side of the freezer paper should face the quilt top. Pin the freezer paper securely to the border.
- On the freezer paper, draw a line from the center border seam-line to the top of the flower pot. Trace the flower pot edge over to the starting point of the vine, then trace the edge of the vine that is closest to the border seam line. When you get to the corner flower, trace its edge as well. Draw a line from the top of the flower up to the edge of the freezer paper.

- The traced shape should look something like the shape at right (or its reverse, if you worked on the left side of the border). Cut the freezer paper along the traced lines to make a placement template for the border vine and corner flowers, similar to the placement templates in Lessons 2, 4 and 6.

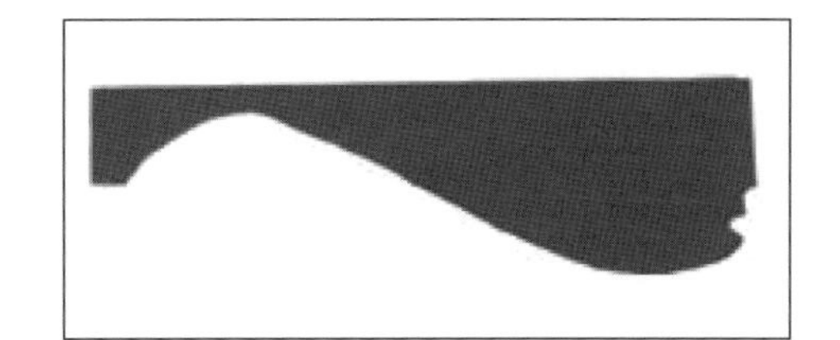

- Now you can use the freezer paper template to place the vine on the rest of the borders. Turn it shiny side up and pin it to the other side of the bottom border. Lay the 1/2" bias vine right along the edge of the template and pin it in place. Move the template to the other borders and pin the other vines in place.
- Refer to the photo to place the rest of the design shapes.
- The side borders are mirror images of each other. You can use another every-day household item — wax paper— to help you place the border elements accurately. Pin the appliqué shapes to one side border, then lay a sheet of wax paper over the entire border. Line up the long edge of the wax paper with the border seam lines. Use a soft-tipped felt pen to trace the appliqué shapes.

  Move the traced wax paper to the other border and pin it in place. You will be able to see through it to place the appliqué shapes in a mirror image of the first border. You also can use this technique to match the right and left sides of the top and bottom borders.

- After you're satisfied with the appliqué placement, remove the basting from the border seams so you can work with each border separately. You will have to unpin the part of the vine that crosses from the side borders into the top and bottom borders. It can't be permanently placed until the quilt borders are sewn back on, so neatly pin it out of the way for now.
- Use the Roxanne's glue to baste the design elements in place.
- Now you get to sew! Machine appliqué the border elements. Stop stitching several inches away from each end of the side borders to allow room for sewing the borders back together.
- Sew the borders onto the quilt again, this time "for real." Glue-baste the corner elements in place, using the freezer paper or wax paper templates again if you need to check placement. Finish the machine appliqué.
- Follow the directions in Lesson 10 for getting the borders wet and taking out the freezer paper.

LESSONS FOR ADAPTING OTHER DESIGNS

We think that making a simple placement template from freezer paper or wax paper is a vast improvement over most of the other methods we've used to place the appliqué pieces accurately.

You may think that basting the borders onto the quilt body, then removing them for appliqué, then sewing them on again sounds like too much work. But we hope you'll try it. It is much faster and easier to sew the borders onto the quilt twice than to machine appliqué four borders that are attached to the quilt.

Lesson 12 — Working with Wool

FABRIC REQUIREMENTS FOR THE *NEW HOME WREATH* WOOL CHAIR PAD

- **Background:** 15" circle of rust-colored wool
- **Wreath and leaves:** 10" x 14" rectangle of green wool
- **Stars:** 8" square of light gold wool
- **Backing:** 1/2 yard of gold plaid cotton

MAKING THE CHAIR PAD

Quiltmakers are attracted to wool because it has a depth of color and texture all its own. We like to use our machine appliqué techniques on wool projects because the nearly invisible stitching gives the completed wool appliqué an antique look.

Traditional wool appliquéd pieces have raw edges. To prevent fraying, start with wool that has been washed in hot water and dried in a hot dryer. The heat "felts" the wool, shrinking it so it doesn't fray very much. You can add an ounce of prevention by cutting the appliqué templates from an iron-on adhesive product.

To make the chair pad,

- Group the pattern pieces by color and trace them onto the iron-on adhesive, keeping in mind the size of wool you will use for each shape. Don't leave room between appliqué shapes for seam allowances. Instead, make the shapes fit together as closely as possible to save space. Trim around each color group but don't cut out the individual pieces.
- Iron the sets of adhesive templates onto the back of the wool, following the manufacturer's directions.
- Cut out each wool shape and remove the protective paper from the adhesive.
- Place the wool shapes onto the wool circle. Iron to fuse them to the circle.
- To machine stitch the edges, use the same appliqué stitch and thread as usual, but make the stitch width about twice as wide so the "bites" will cover enough of the wool's raw edge to securely hold it in place. Also lengthen the stitch length to twice as long as usual.
- Cut two 17-1/2" squares from the gold plaid cotton and mark a a 16" circle on the back of one square. Place the squares right sides together and sew on the marked line, leaving a 2" opening. Trim the seam allowance to 1/4" and turn the circle right-side-out. Slip stitch the opening to close.
- Center the wool appliquéd circle on top of the cotton lining and glue-baste it in place. For a decorative edge, use gold DMC thread and your machine's buttonhole or feather stitch to sew the wool circle to the lining.

New Home Wreath Chair Pad

ONE QUARTER OF DESIGN

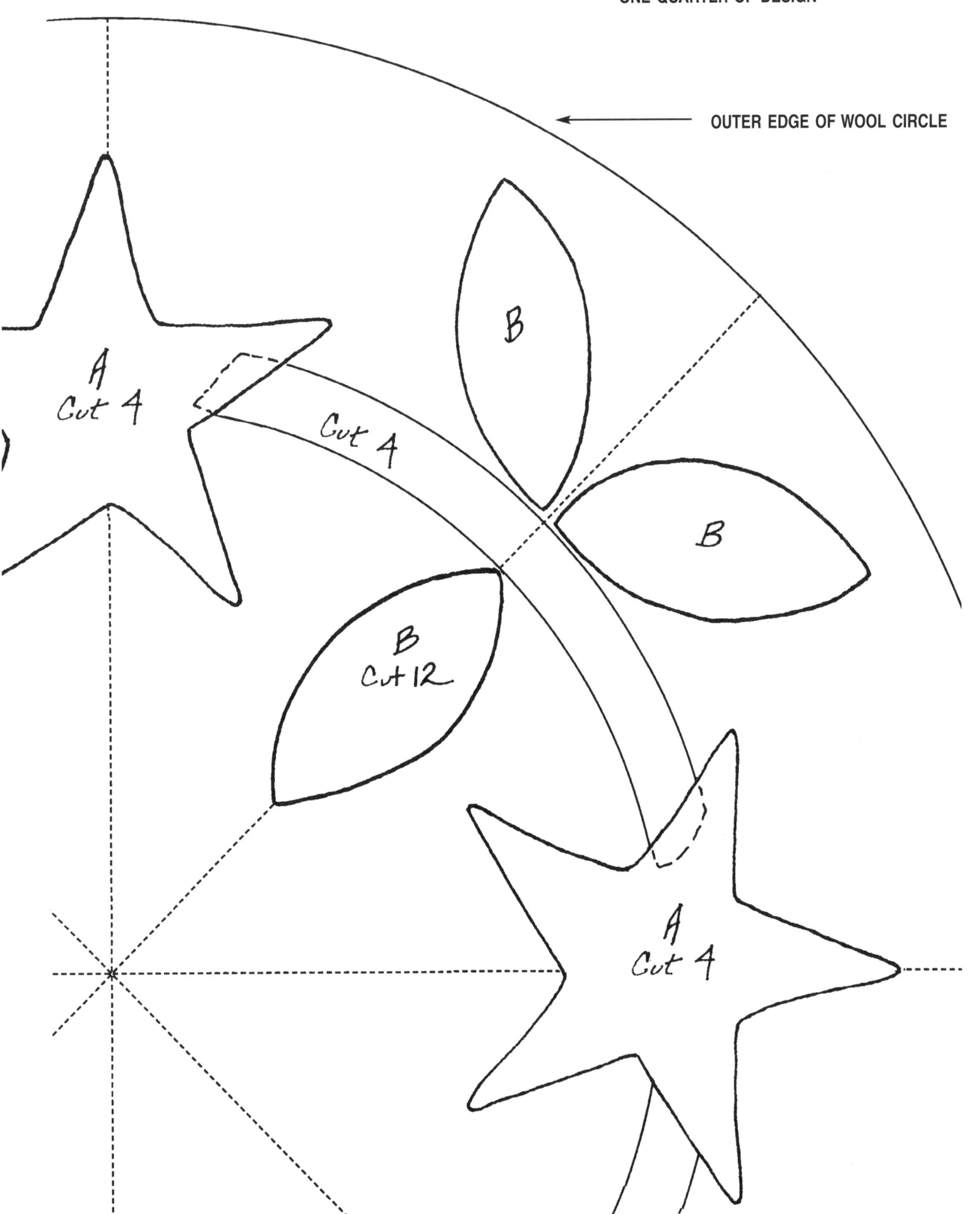

Extra Project — New Century Bouquet

FABRIC REQUIREMENTS FOR THE *NEW CENTURY BOUQUET,* TO FRAME OR QUILT

- **Background:** fat-quarter of light-colored fabric, to be trimmed to 16-1/2" x 20-1/2" after appliqué is complete
- **Open-work basket and flag poles:** 10" x 14" rectangle
- **Flag stripes:** 7" square
- **Flag star field:** 3" x 9" rectangle
- **Flower B:** 5" square
- **Flower center A:** 2-1/2" square
- **Berries:** 1-1/2" x 7-1/2" rectangle
- **Bias Vine:** 6" square
- **Stem and calyx D:** 4" x 7" rectangle
- **Flower bud:** 2" square

MAKING THE APPLIQUÉ PICTURE

After our work on the book *Fat-Quarter Fancywork*, we couldn't resist adding a fat-quarter project to this book. Refer to the Quilt Sampler Lessons for instruction in preparing and stitching the appliquéd block. A pattern placement note: The center flagpole is 9" tall above the basket's center spoke.

We pinned the seam allowance of the finished appliqué block to the sides of a 16" x 20" piece of foam-core board and bought a ready-made 16" x 20" frame. You could quilt your picture instead, if you wish.

New Century Bouquet

SEE THE QUILT SAMPLER LESSONS FOR FULL PATTERN PIECES. PUT THE BOUQUET IN THE OPEN-WORK BASKET FROM LESSON 7.

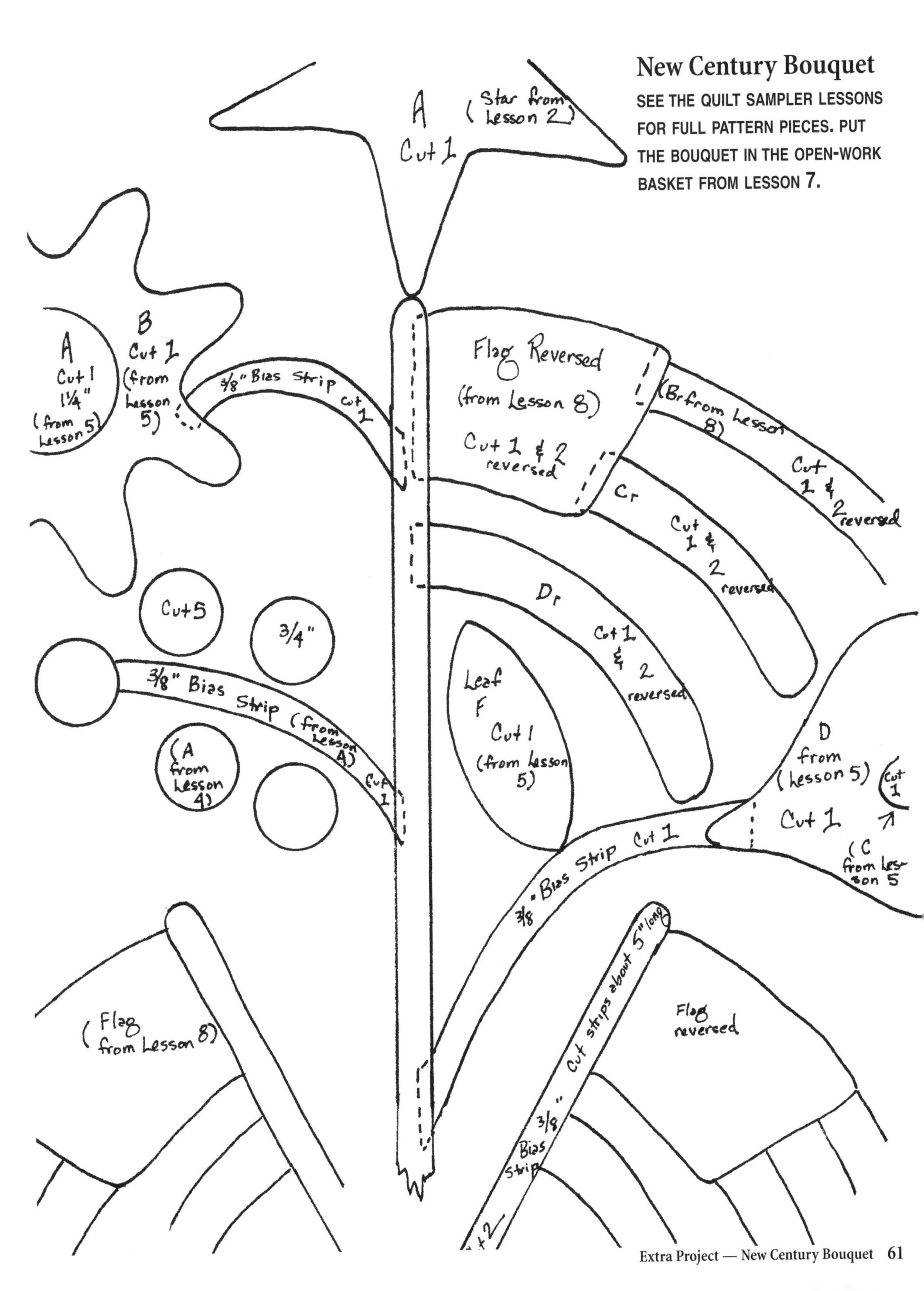

Easy appliqué dresses your table with a bright desert sunset
37" x 15"

Extra Project — Cactus Rose Table Runner

FABRIC REQUIREMENTS

- **Background:** 1/2 yard
- **Scallops:** 1/4 (long quarter) if you make both scallops from the same fabric. Buy more if you want to cut a plaid on the bias like our sample. We bought 1/2 yard for the top border and cut the bottom scallop from a different 1/8 yard of fabric.
- **Cactus appliqué pieces:** Large scraps of six to ten different greens and small scraps of red, purple and yellow for the cactus flowers

MAKING THE TABLE RUNNER

- Cut a 15-1/2" by 37-1/2" rectangle for the background
- Cut two strips of freezer paper 37" x 2-1/4" for the scallops. Fold the freezer paper in half and half again, accordion style. Trace the 9-1/4" unit for the scallop on the top and cut paper-doll fashion.

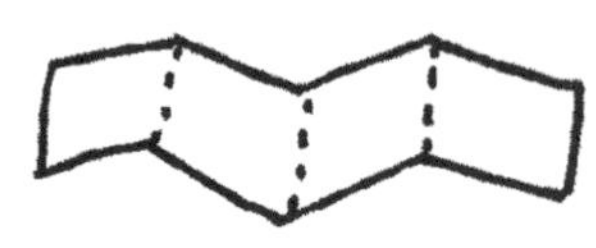

- Press the freezer paper to the scallop fabric and cut out with a 1/4" seam allowance all the way around. Glue under the seam allowances on the wavy edges.
- Position the scallops on the top and bottom of the background and pin in place.
- Cut the templates for the cactus as directed in the pattern. See Lesson 1 for the pattern pieces. Two cactus are just like the pattern in Lesson 1. The placement pattern for the other two cactus is shown at right.

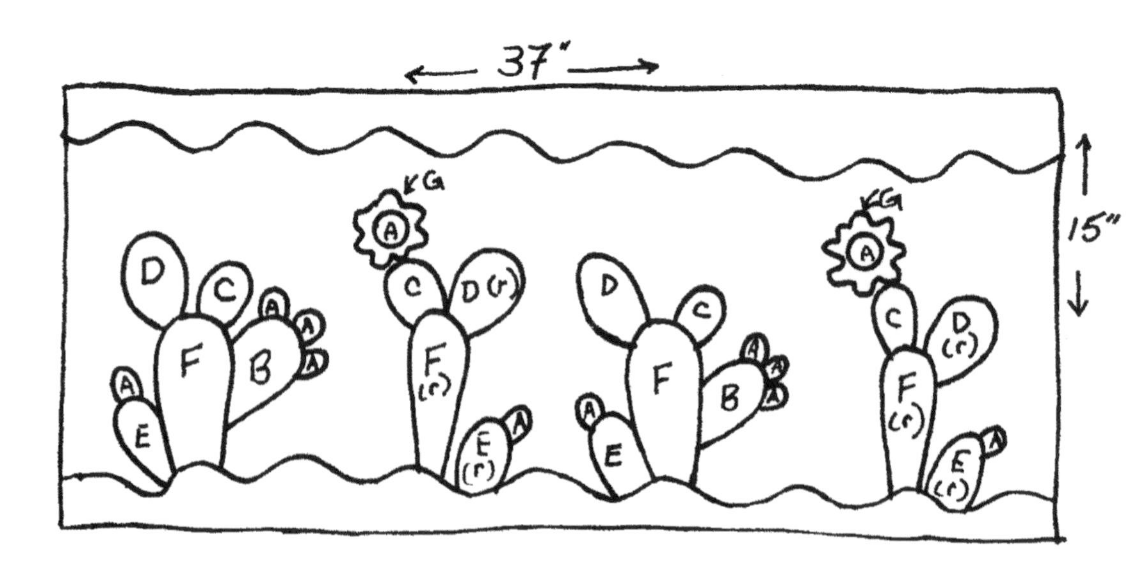

Cactus Rose Table Runner

PLACEMENT GUIDE FOR NEW CACTUS. SEE LESSON 1 FOR PATTERN PIECES AND ANOTHER CACTUS PLANT.

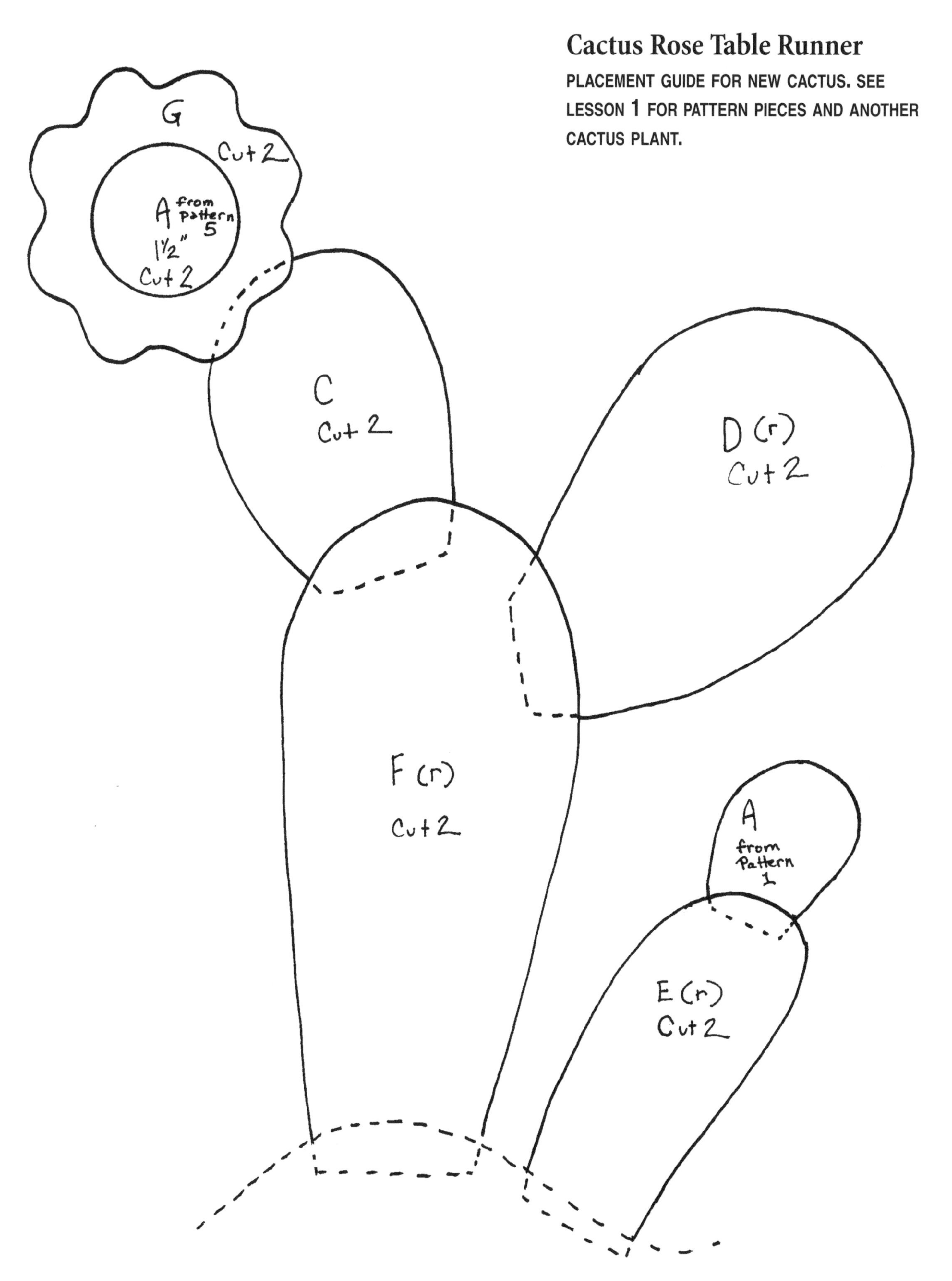

Credits

Our thanks go to Jean Stanclift, who helped us machine appliqué the sampler quilts. Also to Lori Kukuk and Dana Davis, who machine quilted the sampler quilts with such artistry. Lori quilted the cover quilt, *New Century Garden.* Dana quilted its mate, *New Century Sampler.*

SUNFLOWER PATTERN CO-OPERATIVE

Barbara Brackman and Karla Menaugh founded the Sunflower Pattern Co-operative in 1999 to produce quilt patterns inspired by historically significant quilts and other needlework. Our plan was to encourage other quilt artists to design projects as well. We have been proud to have published quilt designs by Kathleen Glasco, Pam Mayfield, Cherie Ralston, Jean Stanclift, and Shirley and Shirlene Wedd.

The Sunflower line of quilt patterns includes special series on quilts from the Civil War and classic crib quilts. All the patterns offer history notes written by Barbara, quilt historian and author of *Quilts from the Civil Wa*r and *Civil War Women, Creating Your Family Quilt, Prairie Flower: A Year on the Plains,* and *Clues in the Calico,* as well as the *Encyclopedia of Pieced Quilt Patterns* and *Encyclopedia of Appliqué.* Another series, ***Patchwork Pals,*** is intended to offer beginning patterns that adults and children can produce together. Earlier this year, Cherie, Barbara and Karla collaborated on the book *Fat-Quarter Fancywork.*

To see other publications from Sunflower Pattern Co-operative, ask at your local quilting store, check our website at quiltsunflower.com or write to us at the address below.

PMB C-237, 3115 W. SIXTH ST., LAWRENCE, KS 66049
(785) 843-9233, FAX: (785) 832-1815
E-MAIL: KCMENAUGH@SUNFLOWER.COM
BARBARA BRACKMAN AND KARLA CARNEY MENAUGH, OWNERS